the
music teacher's *handbook*

the complete resource for all
instrumental and singing teachers

Faber Music • 3 Queen Square • London WC1N 3AU
in association with
Trinity Guildhall • 89 Albert Embankment • London SE1 7TP

Foreword

Teaching music is a demanding job in so many ways. One has to be able to inspire, motivate and cajole pupils as they meet the many challenges of learning to become a musician. Each student comes from a unique background and they will have particular aspirations and needs. In addition to the professional requirements, teaching is hard work, can be exhausting and stressful – yet it can also be extremely rewarding.

By offering a series of topics, each from a different specialist in their own particular field of education, *The Music Teacher's Handbook* aims to arm the music teacher with a range of practical strategies to overcome the issues they commonly face. It is not intended as a comprehensive or exhaustive textbook on all facets of teaching and learning, but rather a stimulating, interesting reference guide. Each chapter focuses on a particular topic, some containing specific photocopiable activities for students to work through, others setting out more general philosophies and ideas for the teacher.

This book gives new insights into teaching and how people learn, and suggests alternative strategies for teachers to try out. Each pupil's achievement and understanding of music will be greatly influenced not only by their teacher's specific skills and knowledge but by his/her flexibility in tailoring a range of teaching approaches to suit them. After all, students always learn most effectively when they enjoy what they are doing!

Mark Stringer
Director of Performing Arts Examinations, Trinity Guildhall

Please note that when referring to instrumentalists and instrumental teachers we are including pianists and singers.

© 2005 by Faber Music Ltd and Trinity College *London*
First published in 2005 by Faber Music Ltd
in association with Trinity College *London*
3 Queen Square London WC1N 3AU
Cover design by Sue Clarke
Cover illustration by Vikki Liogier
Music setting by Stave Origination
Printed in England by Caligraving Ltd
All rights reserved

ISBN 0-571-52330-7

To buy Faber Music or Trinity publications or to find out about the full range of titles available please contact your local music retailer or Faber Music sales enquiries:

Faber Music Ltd, Burnt Mill, Elizabeth Way, Harlow CM20 2HX
Tel: +44 (0)1279 82 89 82   Fax: +44 (0)1279 82 89 83

sales@fabermusic.com fabermusic.com trinitycollege.co.uk

Contents

The psychology of teaching
by Lucinda Mackworth-Young

Understanding pupils

Can you remember how you felt on your way to a first music lesson with a new teacher? What did you hope for, need or dread from the teacher? And from any fellow pupils? Recall particularly your deep, non-rational feelings ('What I'm really hoping is …' or 'It'll be the end of the world if…').

Emotions

New situations bring both excitement and anxiety. Usually, the older the pupil the more the anxiety. There may be anxiety about finding the teaching room, being late and whether the teacher or group will be welcoming. There may be hopes about being found good enough (preferably remarkable, wonderful!) and fears about being found wanting. These feelings exist at a deep and non-rational level, beneath rational surface appearances, and so may easily be underestimated by us. In particular 'not being able to do it' can feel very threatening to pupils – as though the ground is giving way beneath their feet. Common defenses against such anxiety are:

- Evading lessons or practice: it can feel better not to try, than try and fail.
- Arriving late or making excuses to leave early.
- 'Forgetting' the music.
- Engaging us in distracting chatter.
- Fidgeting, attending to anything except the given task.
- 'Going stupid': being unable to understand a word of what is being said, switching off.
- Rushing in to play before being ready, racing ahead out of control.
- Refusing to try, being unco-operative.
- Being impatient (slamming the piano lid down), angry, aggressive or tearful.
- Especially if in a group: keeping very quiet hoping not to be noticed, hiding behind bravura ('Of course I can do it! Piece of cake!'), being disruptive or nastily competitive.
- Giving up (running away).

Pupil and teacher: inner child and parent?

Whether at the age of six or 66, pupils place us above themselves and in so doing they key into their 'inner child', feeling dependent on us and powerless.

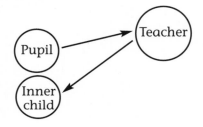

In placing us above themselves they transfer onto us the role of 'parent', all powerful and omnipotent, needing our care and interest for their (musical) survival, and fearing our criticism and neglect which is (musical) death to them.

So not only do pupils fear they might not be able to do it, but they also fear that we will expose, annihilate and cast them out.

Knowing what's going on inside their heads

The extent to which pupils invest us with such power, and whether they see us as predominantly caring or critical, depends on what they are already saying to themselves inside their heads (their 'inner parent'). Inner parents are formed through the internalisation of real parents, care-givers and teachers, and determine:

- Self-concept.
- How they believe 'everyone' sees them.
- What they hear, see and feel about themselves from 'everyone', including us.
- Our own response to them.
- Their 'inner resource' – or stickability at difficult tasks.

Take two pupils, Emily and Carl, starting lessons with a new teacher:

As an infant and young child Emily heard, saw and felt messages from parents, carers and teachers such as: 'You are wonderful, you can succeed.' She internalised these and so developed a caring and supportive inner parent. She unconsciously projects this onto her new music teacher feeling sure that he will feel the same about her as 'everyone' does. So she enters the room with an excited smile – to which her teacher immediately responds positively, feeling sure that lessons with Emily will be a pleasure, which confirms Emily in her self-concept. During the course of lessons Emily's teacher praises and encourages her. She easily hears it as she is already praising and encouraging herself. When she hits a hard patch she sticks with it, saying to herself: 'You can do this, you can succeed!'.

Carl heard, saw, felt and internalised messages such as: 'You don't really matter. You'll never be able to do it, the others are much better than you.' His resulting inner parent is critical and undermining. As he projects it onto his new teacher, he enters the room anxiously, defensively, frowning and with a hint of hostility. This is such a habit of his that he is completely unaware of both how he is feeling and how he appears. As soon as she sees him, his new teacher feels anxious and threatened (see 'Feeling their feelings' below) and finds it very hard to be as warm and welcoming as she normally is. During the course of lessons she praises and encourages him, but he can't take it in because he's already telling himself he's useless, and through projection he believes that's what 'everyone' (including her) really thinks. When he hits a hard patch he's so sure he won't be able to do it that he uses every defence possible to avoid even trying. Before long he's given up, confirmed in his belief that he's no good and no-one really cares.

Feeling their feelings

The way pupils enter their first lesson says much more about them, their inner parent, transferences and projections, than it does about us and our teaching. A pupil who enters with an excited smile is telling us about a positive self-belief and musical expectations. One who enters with a frown and hint of hostility is telling us about very different self-belief and expectations. It is also important for us to notice that they evoke different responses from us, so that we can control our responses and maintain a warm welcome even in the face of the frowner (who would otherwise only have his negative beliefs confirmed by our response).

It can be helpful to realise that our own feelings may actually be telling us how our pupils are feeling as feelings travel gut to gut, by-passing thinking. So, when we find ourselves feeling any emotion in lessons: excitement, appreciation and magic – or anxiety, threat, confusion and helplessness, it is very likely that the pupil will be feeling the same. For example, if we are feeling: 'I'll never be able to teach this, the pupil must be thinking I'm a useless teacher,' we could actually be picking up the pupil's feelings of: 'I'll never be able to play this, the teacher must be thinking I'm useless'. This is called counter-transference.

What they need from us:

In order to contain their learning anxiety (which our very presence, by their transference, may provoke) and encourage their inner resource, it can be helpful if we, in a similar way to parents:

- Welcome their arrival warmly and have a pleasant teaching environment.
- Have deep faith in their musical spirit whether or not it is apparent: if we believe in it they can more readily see and contact it for themselves.
- Attend to them, having our mind around them, making them feel safe – just as parents have their mind and arms around infants.
- Teach positively, praising, encouraging and helping them realise they can do it – perhaps because they've already done it, for example: 'That *staccato* you did there was lovely. Now apply that to this passage!'
- Criticise rarely: sometimes criticism is necessary to shock a pupil into action, but this only works if the teacher-pupil relationship is strong enough and the pupil wants to work to regain the temporarily lost approval. Otherwise it is likely to be felt as an attack, and the pupil may defend himself by not turning up.
- Encourage them to grow towards musical independence, developing an adult/adult rather than parent/inner child teacher-pupil relationship.

Understanding learning: how do you learn?

Through internalisation and internal construction

We learn through internalising information and skills. We internalise through making sense of, linking in with and building onto our existing internal structure. It involves both right and left brain and every possible sense and faculty, in particular in music, aural, kinaesthetic, visual and imaginative skills.

Using the right brain

Infants and young children, experimenters and discoverers learn through doing, then understanding. This is a right-brained, holistic and intuitive approach, characterised by starting with the whole and working towards the particular. It is associated with hearing (aural skills), feeling and imagination, and includes the perception and expression of music. It tends not to be conscious.

Using the left brain
Older children (varying from child to child but generally by the age of 14) and adults, logical thinkers and analysers, learn through understanding then doing. This is a left-brained, step-by-step, methodical approach, characterised by starting from the particular and moving to the whole. It is associated with seeing (visual skills), thinking, analysing and language, so includes 'knowing about' music. It is conscious.

In lessons
In musical terms a right-brained approach would be to learn to sing and move to music, to play by ear and improvise, and to explore and express musical feeling and imagery. A left-brained approach would be to learn to play a piece of music through reading the written note, perhaps first by counting and clapping the rhythm, then identifying note names, then playing it. Technical work, because of its conscious, step-by-step nature is predominantly left-brained, but bodily movement requires both sides of the brain as the right side of the brain operates the left side of the body and vice versa. Interestingly, and perhaps because of this, it is well developed kinaesthetic skills that can help a left-brained sight-reader to play by ear and improvise, and a right-brained player-by-ear to sight read.

As both right and left-brained skills are needed it can be helpful to know which to use when. In general:
- If there is a feeling of chaos, confusion and muddle in a lesson ('What on earth am I doing?') it can be helpful to use clearly defined, step-by-step left-brained tasks.
- If the lesson is feeling stretched and dry ('I'll never get there') it can be helpful to get into musical feeling and imagination – perhaps just having a good play through.

In practice
Whereas lessons (particularly conventional note-reading based lessons) tend to be left-brained – teachers having a lot of 'know how' which they impart step-by-step – practice tends to be right-brained. Pupils, especially young ones and novices, tend just to play through the music to 'see how it goes', consciously or unconsciously avoiding anything that requires putting on the brakes, changing into left-brained gear and tackling difficulties!

For performance
However, in order to perform reliably we all need to know what we are doing clearly and consciously – with our left brains. How often are we able to play so well at home (in our relaxed, less conscious right-brained mode) but have it all fall apart under the self-conscious-making pressure of a lesson, let alone a more formal performance? 'It went alright at home' is a familiar cry!

Using a variety of skills
For the deepest security, all music, scales and pieces (especially all difficult passages) need to be known in the following ways:
Aurally:
- Knowing the sound of every note, part and chord to be played.

- Singing and whole body movements (clapping, stepping, moving) are good ways to internalise the pulse, rhythm, melody, harmony, phrasing, character and mood.

Kinaesthetically:

- Sensing and enjoying the feel of every note so the muscles know exactly what to do and all tension is eliminated.
- Practising slowly, warmly and firmly.
- Hands separately and together (because the right side of the body is operated by the left hemisphere and vice versa this is helpful to practise on nearly all instruments although wind players will want to do it without blowing).
- Feet separately and together (pianists, organists, percussionists).
- Embouchure separately from fingers (brass and wind players).
- Words (left brain) separately from melody (right brain) (singers).
- Without sound: keyboard players on a digital piano with the sound turned off.
- String players without using the bow.
- Using distorted rhythms, where ♩♩ becomes ♩.♩ and ♪♪♩ becomes ♩.♪♩

Visually:

- Reading and understanding everything on the written page.
- Knowing the look of the notes being played on the instrument.
- Knowing the architecture: sections, phrases, keys, chords.
- Being able to visualise playing the music, inwardly hearing, feeling and seeing it (without the written music if performing from memory).

Uniting the skills

It is important to practise at the speed of no mistakes, so that the ears, fingers and eyes all feel comfortably united and in control rather than wildly hoping for the best, and in this way it all sinks in very deeply. Above all, singing the counts whilst playing helps integrate right and left brain and aural, kinaesthetic and visual skills. (Wind players can sing the counts whilst fingering but not blowing.)

Focusing on success

As far as possible (being alert to when they have 'had enough' or feel 'too full'), we need to practise any new skills with pupils in lessons until they are internalised. They practise when they can play it, don't they!

Teacher or pupil-directed lessons?

How were you taught? Did your teacher do all the teaching?

As teachers, it is a common misconception of ours to feel that we have to do all the teaching, as though this ensures our pupils' learning. But learning is internalisation. The only person who can internalise is the person whose internal space it is. Essentially, therefore, we can only teach our pupils to teach themselves.

Teaching in response to pupils

Given this, it is important that we teach in response to our pupils, noticing whether they are engaged in their learning, in which case an important learning process is happening, whether we are giving them enough time and space for this process (pupil-directed learning), or whether they need their learning to be more appetising and digestible (teacher-directed learning).

Noticing the quality and direction of energy in lessons

To help us know how to teach, we need to be in touch with the quality and direction of energy between ourselves and our pupils:

> Bring to mind a recent lesson that went very well. Describe or draw the quality and direction of energy between teacher and pupil.

Good lessons have a mutual flow of energy between teacher and pupil, perhaps something like this:

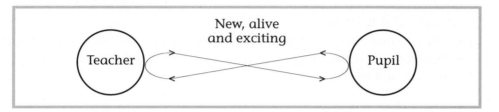

In such lessons there's a sense that everything is new, exciting and alive. Both teacher and pupil feel free to take the initiative and respond to the other's ideas. We find ourselves teaching something we didn't know we knew, or saying something in a way which sheds light even for us. It is, literally, creation in action.

> Now bring to mind a lesson or two that did not go so well and describe or draw the quality and direction of energy:

Perhaps you felt:
1   You were trying very hard but the pupil was not responding – and the less the pupil responded the harder you tried? Or:
2   Both teacher and pupil seemed caught in a feeling of uncertainty and helplessness?

Using pupil-directed learning

In the first example above, it was likely to be the teacher trying so hard which increasingly put the pupil off. He probably felt railroaded down a path he didn't want to take, pushed, rushed, muddled and stupid. In cases like these we need to elicit pupils' energy by:
•   Finding out about their musical interests, ambitions and dreams.
•   Getting them to set their own long and short-term goals.
•   Helping them take responsibility for their learning by asking them to:

a   identify what they played well – and why

b   identify and decide how to tackle their problems.

By enabling pupils to learn what they want to learn, in their way and at their speed, pupil-directed learning redresses frustrations and blocked energy and can also reduce anxiety.

Using teacher-directed learning

In the second example (above), the teacher needed to recognise that both were caught in negative countertransference, but that it was up to her (as 'parent') to take the lead and direct energy by:

• Taking charge.
• Breaking tasks down into bite-sized portions.
• Imparting skills and techniques in appetising and digestible ways.
• Changing activity to something the pupil enjoys and can do.

Teacher-directed learning enables pupils to learn something new and learn how to learn (we do it with them until the new skill is internalised). It redresses helpless and stuck energy, and can also reduce anxiety!

Lightness and humour

In both instances the lesson needed to be more fun! Injecting a lightness of touch, a sense of humour and playing enjoyably (letting rip with the right brain!) can all help.

Involving parents/carers

A good teacher-parent/carer relationship can greatly assist successful learning. For this we need to remember that:

• First impressions are powerful and long-lasting: whether the first contact is over the telephone or face-to-face we need to reassure parents/carers of our care, interest and professionalism.
• We need to be clear about lessons, fees, cancellation procedures, whether or not the parent/carer sits in on lessons (depending on the teacher's preferences, the particular dynamic and what best supports and motivates the pupil).
• We need to discuss a realistic practice schedule.
• We need to welcome feedback and ongoing discussion.

When in difficulty

We need to arrange a meeting or telephone call to discuss difficult situations. If suddenly accosted by an irate parent (as may easily happen before the teacher is aware that anything is wrong), for example: 'Mary has not made nearly as much progress as I'm expecting! Her friends are all on Grade 2!' it can be very helpful to:

• Resist the urge to react defensively.
• Gently reflect back what you've heard: 'Mary is not making as much progress as you'd expected...her friends are on Grade 2?' (Feeling heard by the teacher takes the aggressive wind out of parents/carers' sails and enables calm discussion.)
• Listen and accept the parents/carers' feelings without judgement.
• Ask questions to find out as much as possible about their point of view.
• Give appreciation where possible (thanks and compliments are great diffusers!).

- Gently explain your own point of view.
- Invite discussion without being attached to a particular outcome.
- Trust that a mutually satisfying solution will arise out of the discussion.

Useful phrases include:
'Thank you so much for telling me… it's very helpful to know…'
'I'm wondering whether…'
'How would you feel if…'
And if stuck or floored: 'May I think about that… and get back to you?'

Above all, trust yourself, trust the other person, trust the process.

Further reading
Tuning in: Practical Psychology for Musicians who are Teaching, Learning and Performing
Lucinda Mackworth-Young (ISBN 0953948501)
musicmindmovement@btinternet.com

Lucinda Mackworth-Young
MA(PsychEd) TCL(Hons) LTCL(Piano) LTCL(Clar) Consultant in Psychology for Musicians, concert pianist, teacher, lecturer and writer.

© 2005 by Lucinda Mackworth-Young

Planning for success

by Nick Beach

Before getting into the business of planning, let's take a step back and consider some of the issues surrounding this somewhat controversial subject. In recent years there have been many assumptions made about planning and most of these take the view that instrumental/vocal teachers and their pupils would benefit from the sort of planning regime adopted by classroom teachers. This is a questionable assumption. There are some major differences between what instrumental teachers (including those working with small groups) are trying to do compared with classroom teachers. For a start, instrumental pupils choose to take lessons – they don't have to be there – and we are usually dealing with small groups at most. For the classroom teacher a plan is often a matter of survival – chaos may break out if there is any break in the flow of the lesson!

Planning a good or bad lesson?

If we are going to look at the issue of planning for instrumental/vocal lessons let's do it from the point of view of what it will do for the pupil. Will they get a better experience from a planned lesson than they would otherwise? It is probably as easy to plan a bad lesson as a good one, so the answer could well be 'no'.

Planning will not make your teaching better and will not make your pupils happier!

Some will inevitably link the idea of planning with a fixed curriculum and timetable for development – statements such as 'by the end of the first term pupils will be able to…' spring to mind. Such devices are engineered to produce failures – if the 'average' child will get to this stage in two terms then presumably 'below average' pupils will fail in the attempt. Such thinking should have no place in instrumental/vocal teaching. Our role should be to make music with children and help them do it better. The speed of development is not an issue as long as the pupil is fulfilled in his/her music making.

Why plan at all?

So, if there is little intrinsic merit in planning for its own sake why should we bother with it at all? It is possible to make some more positive statements about the underlying principles of planning. When we look at the attributes of good teachers we see some patterns. A good teacher has:

- A clear understanding of the musical concepts they are helping children to understand, along with some ideas about the ordering of those concepts.
- The ability to give lessons a clear and logical structure.
- Consideration of the practical side. Good lessons need resources: music, games and materials.
- Some form of record-keeping: a teacher who knows what their pupils have been working on for the last few weeks in some detail can give a clearer focus to the lesson.

So how might we develop these positive aspects of the planning process without dragging ourselves down with a cumbersome and inflexible curriculum for our instrument?

Planning for the individual

If you put a group of teachers of any instrument in a room together and ask them to agree the order in which you should teach the various elements needed to play their instrument there will be an animated discussion! There are no fixed answers, but what is vital is that in all our planning the pupil remains at the heart of the matter.

Pupils need different things at different times; some will be ready to do things at different times to others. Are we really to say to the pupil who comes in bursting to play some high notes 'Sorry, we don't do those until lesson 13'? What we need to understand are the concepts themselves, along with any clear progression routes. Here is a very valuable exercise recommended to any teacher:

- Consider the basic overarching aims you have for your pupils. The chances are you will finish up with a list of development areas looking more or less like this:

  Technique
  Musical understanding
  Expressive development
  Knowledge

- You may have five areas, you may have three, they may vary from those shown – no matter. Take each of these areas and divide it further into component parts. For example:

Technique

fingering
bowing
embouchure
lip flexibility
dynamic range
tonal range
  and so on.

- Now take one of these areas and consider whether some things need to be in place before others can be considered. For example, work on written notation is irrelevant to pupils before they have some concept of pulse and pitch. Consideration of the techniques required to play loud and soft is irrelevant before pupils understand the musical impact of playing dynamics.
- Remember: some of the ordering we insist on in our teaching is artificially imposed and we should beware of it. Why do we so often start in the middle of the piano and in first position on a string instrument? There is nothing intrinsically more difficult with the extremes of the instrument and the more imaginative beginners' materials encourage investigation of these areas.

Creating lesson aims

Now we have a basic skill set for success on our instrument which can inform and assist our teaching. The next stage is to turn it into aims for our lessons, an exercise which can yield huge benefits. In many unsuccessful lessons the sole aim is to learn the set pieces. Many teachers do not have an aim beyond 'by the end of this lesson my pupil(s) will be able to get through piece number 5 in the book'. This is not a useful aim and is likely to result in a note-bashing session, which is discouraging for both pupil and teacher.

1. Establish the timescale

The most useful period over which to set aims is a medium term one: over about six lessons or half a term. This allows for the set aims to be approached in a variety of ways and gives the pupil a chance to develop and grow in these areas. It also encourages a meaningful assessment at the end of the period as to the degree to which the aims have been met.

2. Establish your aims

The next step in our planning exercise is to set the aims for our pupils. You already have a list from which to select and it would be tempting to get stuck in and start setting aims left, right and centre – I would urge caution! These are currently *your* aims and they may or may not match those of your pupils. It is very difficult, if not impossible, to teach someone something they don't want to learn. It is very easy to teach someone something they do want to learn.

3. Discuss the aims with your pupil

My recommendation is that, at the start of each planning period, you take ten minutes out of your lesson time to sit down and discuss with your pupils to what extent they think they achieved their aims for the last period and what they think their aims should be for the coming one. Once the pupil has ownership of the aims, you are half way there – and you will probably be surprised that they pick the ones you would have picked yourself. Naturally, you may want to suggest some extra ones – but if you meet with resistance *try to have the courage to go with your pupil's agenda…*

> Don't be over-ambitious – stick to three or four aims for the period. Think about it – if all our pupils made real progress with three or four fundamental aspects of playing/singing over each six week period we would be very pleased, and they would feel a great sense of achievement.

Achieving the aims

Consider your strategies

Now you have a set of aims which you have agreed with your pupils, what next? Think about some of the strategies you will use to deliver those aims. If your aim is to introduce a new note, extend the pupil's range, or learn some new key signatures, what teaching ideas will you use to do this? What needs to be in place before they can learn this new thing? In the previous exercise you developed your building blocks for teaching – use this to check that everything is in place that needs to be. Then look at specific teaching strategies: games, repertoire, warm-ups, exercises and so on. You will end up with a list of activities that will form the basis of your teaching with these pupils over the six-week period.

Fit within a structure

At the moment we simply have a list of ideas – in order for them to make any sense in a lesson they must fit into some kind of structure. Instrumental/vocal teachers are busy people, often delivering a huge number of lessons each week, so I would recommend that you have a basic structure for your lessons which doesn't vary much. The following is pretty standard:

Basic lesson structure

Very broadly the structure of the lesson can be divided into three main parts. This structure should be the basic framework on which every lesson rests:

Warm-up

The function of this part of the lesson is to take the pupil from what they have been doing prior to the lesson (in a group situation it can be a range of activities) and focus them on music. The instrumental music lesson is not like any other activity in which pupils become involved: you could argue that it is the only activity which links response to aural stimuli (listening), and visual stimuli (reading music or copying the teacher) with a physical activity (playing/singing). Such a change in activity needs to be properly prepared. The other function of the warm-up is a health issue; damage can be done, especially to voices, if warm-up routines are not carried out properly.

Main body of the lesson

This is where the main work is carried out – pieces heard, technical work covered, new skills taught, and so on.

Summary

The old maxim for structuring lessons still holds good: tell them about what you are going to tell them, tell them, and then tell them what you told them. A summary at the end of the lesson is vital to focus the pupil's mind on the work that has been covered during the lesson. It is also the point at which pupils are set work for the coming week.

The practicalities

Now you can hang your teaching strategies on this structure, giving due consideration to lesson balance and progression. But before you can deliver your plans you will need to ensure that you have all the resources demanded by the strategies you are planning to use. These might include music, props, games materials, CD players and so on!

Record keeping

Finally, we acknowledged earlier that teachers who have a clear and detailed idea of what their pupils have been working on for the last few weeks will be better able to provide a clear focus to the lesson. For most teachers who are working with large numbers of pupils this will involve some kind of record keeping system. Clearly there is no place for a time-consuming system here and teachers will use a variety of methods. What is important is fitness for purpose – whatever system you use must tell you not just what the pupil did last week but what was covered in the last few lessons.

A practical approach

Planning is a useful activity as it helps to organise your thoughts and rationalise your approach to teaching. However, you are not going to have the time to design a lesson plan and write it up for every lesson you teach. This is the reason many teachers give for not planning at all. The approach we have outlined could be summarised as follows:

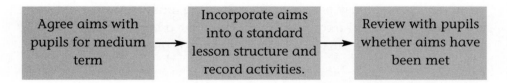

| Agree aims with pupils for medium term | → | Incorporate aims into a standard lesson structure and record activities. | → | Review with pupils whether aims have been met |

Some final thoughts

There will be times when you cannot stick to the plan
- The pupil turns up without music or instrument.
- The plan depended on all the group being there and half are away.
- Your pupil says 'I really want to play this piece I have brought – it's fantastic!'
- Your pupil cries, faints, vomits…

A plan is not a straitjacket but a possible path
Don't be fixated with the plan and miss all the wonderful opportunities that will be presented by your pupils. A plan should open up the lesson, not close it down.

Don't use your plan as a stick to beat your pupils with
'You haven't done enough practice so we are behind on our targets' may induce guilt but guilt doesn't encourage success. 'If you don't practise more you won't meet your targets' will induce fear but fear doesn't encourage success. 'If you reach your targets I'll give you a sticker' is merely bribery. 'This is great work – well done!' will give a good feeling and encourage future success.

Nothing breeds success like success.

Nick Beach
Deputy Director,
Trinity Guildhall
Examinations

An integrated approach

by Philippa Bunting

'It would... seem unwise to base any form of music education more or less exclusively on performing, whether in individual instrumental instruction or in ensembles. The evidence supports the view that students should have access to a range of musical possibilities, including composing and audience-listening. Whenever possible this should be in an integrated way, not with separate teachers. Only then can we be confident that they are able to develop their musical understanding to fuller potential.'
(Keith Swanwick)

Taking the longer view

Whichever instrument we teach and whatever approach we employ, we are above all teachers of music. Sometimes it is easy to get bogged down in the complexities of teaching technique, or in learning repertoire for specific ends such as exams, and forget to sit back and take the longer view. It can seem a challenge to allow time in already squeezed lessons to encourage the kind of deep learning that provides bedrock for a future in music that technical proficiency alone cannot give.

> The kind of teaching that encourages true understanding can take a little longer in the initial stages, but the benefits later on are enormous.

Learning away from the instrument

It is a general principle of learning music that you proceed from the sub-conscious to the conscious: you experience something before you have to intellectualise it. This experience is generally most usefully had away from the instrument in the first instance, using voices and/or body movement so that technical concerns are removed.

Once the concept you are teaching (be it rhythmic, pitch-based, structural, stylistic or expressive) has bedded in, then you can transfer it to the instrument, dealing with any technical issues at this point.

> Sometimes it isn't just a question of teaching something new, but of taking something the body or mind already knows and transferring it into sound.

The examples on the following page show that the advantage of structuring lessons in this way is that technique is clearly approached in the service of musical ends. This is not to say that technique isn't tackled thoroughly, with close attention to issues of posture and avoidance of tension, but that it all stems from musical starting points. Throughout, the focus needs to be on the music, on sound and on personal expression. Succeed in that, and the motivation to take on new skills and techniques will take care of itself.

Concept	Activity	Transfer to instrument	Next step
Minim rest	Walking around the room, stepping a crotchet pulse, stop and invent a gesture that lasts for two beats.	Create a gesture you can perform whilst holding your instrument, and perform it, using the gesture in place of a minim rest.	Work on three and four beat rests.
Perfect fourth	Learn a number of simple songs that include perfect fourths in different contexts, and encourage pupils to recognise them, using whatever language you find appropriate.	Find the interval in various places all over the instrument, transposing as appropriate, and then play the songs learned.	Extend this work to include other perfect intervals.
Binary form	Use recorded music to introduce pieces in this form, and encourage pupils to first show a sense of home and away, and then explore the contrasting characters of the two sections. Use language, movement or visual representation.	Introduce binary form repertoire which is easily and quickly learned, and focus on the technical means of achieving the contrast between the two sections.	Extend work to ABA form, then rondo form.
Phrasing	Taking a known piece, ask the pupil to express the phrasing physically, marking the end of each phrase with a change of direction.	Returning to the instrument, ask the pupil to keep the physical movement in mind when performing the piece.	Further work to refine the sense of extended line.

Choosing appropriate repertoire

Adopting an integrated approach, where musical and technical development proceed hand in hand, will alter your approach to repertoire, particularly in the early stages. With a clear idea of the concepts you want to introduce, you can choose repertoire specifically to support these projects. A dialogue opens up, whereby some repertoire is chosen for the concepts you want to teach, and other repertoire inspires you both to develop creative preparatory exercises and provides a stimulus to further musical discovery.

For example, this simple phrase of music can be explored from all of these angles and more besides:

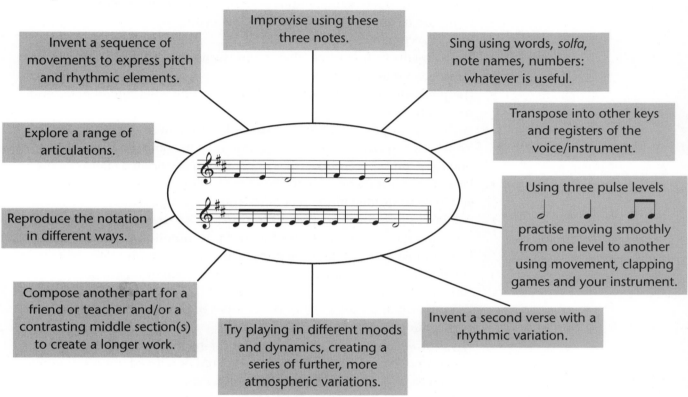

As instrumental teachers we are in a unique position to use our close relationship with our pupils to develop not only their musicianship but their personal qualities as well.

What are the advantages of exploring repertoire from so many different angles?

- Lots of repetition means positive reinforcement.
- Covering many points using one piece of music saves time.
- Exploring material in many different ways ensures thorough musical understanding.
- It's good preparation for a generative, creative approach to practising.
- It encourages pupils to do their own musical problem-solving.
- It fosters a child-centred approach, where pupils have input into their lesson, and are putting forward their own musical ideas.

> Make sure you are continually reframing questions, and presenting the same concepts in different ways and in different contexts, to check that your pupils' understanding is solid and confident.

Further ideas for integrated activities

- Singing a piece before playing it is a good idea, but you can also sing at any point within the piece, or alternate singing and playing, or even do both at once!
- Sing in *solfa*, letter names, finger numbers, rhythm names – whatever you like – and encourage pupils to make up their own words.
- Compose or improvise variations on pieces already learnt, or invent a middle section.
- Use elements from a piece (such as an isorhythm or tone set) as a basis for improvisation exercises.
- Use physical gestures to explore the length of rests, sustained notes and whole phrases.
- Encourage pupils to find 'mood' words like 'dreamily', 'angrily', 'worriedly', 'spikily' to describe the way they are going to play a piece, and focus on the technical ways of achieving the desired effect.
- Play simple games on and off the instrument to explore rhythmic elements contained in the repertoire you are using.
- Ask pupils to reconstruct pieces they already know using rhythm cards and simple staves (building up from graphic notation to using 2 then 5 lines, at first with no clef then introducing their own and later others).
- Encourage pupils to draw pictures to express form or mood, or construct a narrative for a given piece.
- Use miming and mirrors to work on issues of posture and articulation of the joints.
- Physical warm-ups can plant the seeds for even complex technical issues, and also move the body into the kind of relaxed but alert stance needed to play successfully and without tension.
- Encourage pupils to listen widely, talk about their listening critically and bring pieces to the lesson in recorded form to be learned by ear.

> As a rule, much traditional instrumental teaching has favoured the visual approach, focusing on notated music reading. A range of activities in your lessons will help you work with the strengths of pupils whose preferred learning style is auditory or kinaesthetic.

Once repertoire has been mined in these ways, and as many more as your invention and that of your pupils' dictate, it can then act as a reference point for pupil and teacher alike – a shortcut, as it were, to a whole area of musical understanding. It also acts as a springboard into further exploration and invention since musical, as human spontaneity, flourishes when it has a firm basis from which to depart.

Philippa Bunting
MA, Assistant Director
(Academic),
Royal Northern College
of Music

Further reading
Rhythm, Music and Education J. Dalcroze (Best Books ISBN 0722258119)
The National Curriculum for England and Wales DFEE/QCA (HMSO)

The Sounding Symbol G. Odam (Nelson Thornes ISBN 0748723234)

Teaching Music Musically K. Swanwick (RoutledgeFalmer ISBN 0415199360)

Other teaching methods

Here are two teaching methods which use aspects of integrated learning:

Dalcroze Eurhythmics

'The most potent element in music, and the most related to life, is rhythmic movement.'

Émile Jaques-Dalcroze

Dalcroze Eurhythmics is a way of understanding and expressing the elements of music in a physical way through movement of the whole body. This effective and creative approach to musical training for all ages was developed by Émile Jaques-Dalcroze who was a composer, improviser and revolutionary educationalist whose ideas influenced the whole development of music, dance and drama in the twentieth century.

Eurhythmics means 'good rhythm' and the method consists of three disciplines:
- Rhythmics: experiencing the elements of music through movement
- Solfa: aural training based on Kodály
- Instrumental improvisation

An intellectual and aural understanding of musical concepts is essential in performance. Since music-making is a physical activity, the body needs to know what these concepts feel like. In doing Rhythmics the whole body is involved, experiencing and remembering activities and sensations, later to be recalled and expressed when singing or playing. Aural acuity is improved and inner hearing developed. Rhythm becomes more accurate and vital. Communication between the mind and the body is faster leading to improved co-ordination and concentration.

Use of the whole body adds the element of space to those of time and energy and helps one to better understand what is involved in performance. Good tone production, playing or singing with rhythmic vitality, feeling the line of a phrase or the dynamics of a bar time, conveying the form or expressing the emotions of a piece are all improved.

Jane Rivers
Dalcroze Society UK (Inc.)
www.dalcroze.org.uk

The Kodály Approach to Music Education

'A child who plays before he sings may remain unmusical for a lifetime...'

Zoltán Kodály

The principles of music education devised by the Hungarian composer and educator Zoltán Kodály are in essence extremely simple.

Kodály realised that the voice is the most natural instrument and one which we all possess. Singing has a profound effect upon physical, social, emotional and intellectual development, and any concept learned through this internal instrument is learned more thoroughly and with more understanding than if an 'external' instrument is used.

Kodály identified three stages to the learning process:
• The Unconscious Experience
• The Making Conscious
• Reinforcement

In other words:
• Preparation
• Presentation
• Practice

Initially the children learn through the 'mother-tongue' approach; they learn songs and rhymes by imitation. Gradually what they have assimilated unconsciously is made conscious and children learn both the appropriate vocabulary to describe their experience and the written symbol which represents it. In this way, musical literacy is taught in a practical and logical sequence.

Good teaching goes from the simple to the complex in a series of logical steps. The steps are very small which means that success is guaranteed. Success breeds confidence and the desire to learn more.

Children taught music in this way are confident with singing and performing on their own. Their pitching becomes secure and their sense of pulse is strong. Children who are taught Kodály thoroughly and systematically become joyful, rounded, confident musicians – not just instrumentalists.

Cyrilla Rowsell
British Kodály Academy
www.britishkodalyacademy.org

Health and safety

by Nick Beach

*In this chapter we'll consider the safety of what we do as teachers.
'Health and safety' has a rather a bureaucratic ring to it but nonetheless
there are several issues under this heading to which teachers should give
consideration. Some of these concern various physical problems that can
arise from playing an instrument or singing, while others relate to the
teaching environment itself.*

Physical problems

The expectations we have of ourselves as musicians are not dissimilar to
those of an athlete. We take a very specialised set of physical skills and hone
these to as close to perfection as we can manage. The difference is that,
whereas most athletes have access to all the knowledge and equipment needed to ensure the safe development of skills, musicians are usually on their
own. This places a significant responsibility on the shoulders of the teacher
who must help the pupil establish habits from the outset that will foster a
healthy physical approach to the instrument or voice. The teacher must also
be able to recognise the signs of problems starting to arise and know what
to suggest to avoid them turning into something more serious.

> A word of warning here. The very fact of highlighting a problem or
> syndrome can encourage more occurrences of that problem,
> especially amongst highly impressionable teenagers. Whilst teachers
> should be vigilant in spotting the signs of the onset of physical
> problems, sensitive students can easily become obsessed.

The importance of the warm-up
An athlete wouldn't dream of going straight into a demanding physical
activity without warming-up properly first. A warm-up is essential for every
musician before performing, whether in a practice session, a lesson or in
public. This habit should be established from the very first lesson and
students should be encouraged to think of the warm-up as integral to playing or singing.

Clearly the content of the warm-up will differ between different instruments/
voice but the aim will be the same: to ensure that the muscles used in
performance are supple and ready to do their job. A good idea would be to
write out a warm-up regime for pupils in the early stages and insist that it is
the first thing they do each time they practise. A skilfully-designed warm-up
session can also cover some important technical issues. Do note that scales
and arpeggios are not, in themselves, a warm-up. It is no better to launch
into a difficult scale cold than it is to start with a difficult piece. The answer
to the successful warm-up is in a gradual approach, moving from very
simple movements to more demanding ones.

Good posture and technique
The importance of good posture cannot be over-emphasized. It is essential

to realise that it takes time to build up a good technical facility, just as it does to develop stamina. As a teacher, you must constantly monitor your pupils' posture and practice habits in order to achieve a secure technique.

Over-exertion is a recipe for problems, so as well as warming up properly, teachers should ensure that pupils structure their practice well. A pupil who takes regular short breaks to walk around and do a little gentle stretching is less likely to suffer problems. You should also take time to talk to your pupils about their practice environment:

- Do they have the right equipment (do they have a music stand and is it at the correct height and angle)? If a chair/piano stool is necessary is it suitable and at the correct height: discuss with your pupils or their parents how they can check this.
- Do they have enough space to achieve the ideal posture without feeling restricted in their movements?
- Keep an eye on younger pupils' instruments to be sure they are still the correct size.

Don't ignore aches and pains

It is not uncommon for students to complain of aches and pains when playing and these should always be taken seriously. Playing an instrument or singing should never involve discomfort and a huge amount of damage can be done by ignoring these signs and hoping they will go away.

Teachers need to take a calm and balanced approach, considering a range of possibilities followed by possible solutions. The first issue to check is for stresses and strains in the student's technique, but some gentle questioning about practice habits often throws up clues. I particularly remember a student who admitted she practised the violin sitting on the bed with her music on the floor – not a recipe for a sound and stress-free technique! There will be times when more serious problems arise which require specialist help.

Creating a safe teaching environment

Here are a few guidelines to help avoid accidents:

- It is vital to check (annually) the safety of all wiring, plugs and connections and to ensure that trailing leads do not create a hazard.
- Take care to explain the setting up of all equipment, especially electrical equipment.
- Never ask a pupil to lift heavy equipment and enlist help if you aren't sure you can manage.
- Ensure there are procedures for fire and accident reporting and that everyone is aware of them.
- Never share instruments which are put into the mouth.

Sound levels

Some instruments are loud and it is in the nature of good tone production to encourage students to play with a full sound. A trumpet teacher will be encouraging his/her students to develop the sort of sound that will fill a concert hall, but might be teaching in a small practice room. Teachers working with rock and pop bands will be similarly exposed, as could organists. If you are concerned that you are dealing with potentially damaging sound levels there are a number of products which might help, from the humble ear-plug through to sophisticated electronic devices. Don't forget to make your pupils aware of potential damage to the ear as well. More information is available in the extract from the Musicians' Union (UK) factsheet and the websites listed at the end of this chapter.

Child protection

As a teacher, you need to be aware of child protection issues these days, from how to deal with discussions relating to pupils' personal problems to appropriate levels of physical contact, and so on. It is important to abide by the regulations set out by your employer or, for private teachers, to seek advice from your union or professional organisation. For a more detailed listing of child protection issues see page 94.

If you are a private teacher, it is your responsibility to make sure your working practices and facilities meet health and safety standards. If you work for an employer, make sure you are aware of and comply with their health and safety policies. If you're unsure of your position, check with an appropriate professional body.

Nick Beach
Deputy Director,
Trinity Guildhall
Examinations

Further reading

The Athletic Musician: A Guide to Playing without Pain Barbara Paull, Christine Harrison (The Scarecrow Press Inc ISBN 0810833565)

Essential Musical Intelligence Louise Montello (Quest Books ISBN 083560814X)

Further information

Musicians' Union: www.musiciansunion.org.uk There are many useful factsheets on health and safety matters for musicians, available to members. Extracts from two of their factsheets have been reproduced in this article, with permission.

For information on hearing loss for musicians: www.hearnet.com or www.sensaphonics.com/articles/musicians.html

Repetitive Strain Injury Awareness: www.rsi.websitehosting-services.co.uk

The Alexander Technique has a long history of helping instrumentalists and singers to perform with less stress and likelihood of injury. By helping musicians improve the quality of the physical movements involved in playing an instrument or singing, the Alexander Technique also helps improve the quality of the music itself.
The Society of Teachers of Alexander Technique: www.stat.org.uk
The Complete Guide to the Alexander Technique: www.alexandertechnique.com

Musicians' Union UK factsheet: Noise awareness for musicians

Musicians can grow so used to high sound levels that they accept them as a natural part of their working life and therefore may underestimate the risks. In fact, you may not even be aware that your hearing is deteriorating until it is too late. The inner ear is damaged, which causes an irreversible deafness that cannot be corrected using a hearing aid. The risk depends on how loud the sound is and how long you are exposed to it.

If you are exposed to high noise levels at work, your employer should arrange for you to have your hearing tested regularly, by experts. Your employer must keep records of the results, make sure you are told about your results and what they mean and ensure that you get medical advice if you have hearing loss.

Checklist
• Identify if you have a noise problem by doing your own survey or questionnaire of colleagues.

- Are any of your colleagues experiencing hearing problems, ie difficulty in hearing normal conversation, tinnitus (persistent ringing in the ears), or sensitivity to sounds?
- Ask your employer for a copy of the noise assessment that should have been carried out.
- Ask your employer for a noise assessment to be done if one has not already been carried out.
- Ensure that your employer is implementing a planned noise reduction/prevention programme and you and your members are consulted about it also.
- Are suitable ear protectors available on request?
- Is audiometry available?
- Are noise hazard warning signs in place where hearing protection is required?

Musicians' Union UK factsheet: Overuse/misuse injuries (commonly known as RSI)

The term Repetitive Strain Injury (RSI) is not in itself a medical diagnosis. It is used incorrectly to describe a number of named musculoskeletal conditions (such as Tenosynovitis, Cramp of the Hand, Tendinitis, etc.) as well as 'diffuse RSI' which is more difficult to define. These may be occupational in origin. RSI conditions occur in both upper and lower limbs as well as effecting the spine in various areas, which in turn can cause referred pain in the limbs, making diagnosis difficult. Symptoms of numbness, tingling, sharp pain, dull ache, weakness, loss of grip and restricted movement of limbs can render people incapable of carrying out the simplest of tasks, at home or at work. Lack of accurate diagnosis and access to appropriate treatment further exacerbates the condition.

Risk factors:

- Repetitive work, requiring the use of fast frequent movements for prolonged periods. This repetition may not allow sufficient time for recovery and can cause muscle fatigue due to depletion of energy and a build up of metabolic waste materials. Repeated loading of joints and soft tissues may be associated with inflammation.
- Working postures can increase the risk of injury when they are awkward and/or held for prolonged periods in a static or fixed position.
- Awkward postures where a body part is used well beyond its neutral position. When awkward postures are adopted, additional muscular effort is needed to maintain body positions, as muscles are less efficient at the extremes of the joint range. The resulting friction and compression of soft tissues structures can also lead to injury.
- Static postures occur when a part of the body is held in a particular position for extended periods of time without the soft tissues being allowed to relax. When holding an instrument it is likely that the hands and arms are in a static posture. Muscles held in static postures fatigue very quickly.
- Duration of exposure: it is presumed that the majority of musculoskeletal disorders are cumulative in nature. Therefore when exposure time is increased the risk of injury is increased. When parts of the body undertake work for periods without rest, there may be insufficient time for recovery, so planning of work-rest cycles is important.

Prevention:

- The first stage in protecting yourself is knowing when and where you are in danger.
- Each instrument has its own set of risks – be sure you know where yours are.
- Establish proper performance habits.
- Maintain correct posture.
- Examine and adjust your technique.
- Develop warm-up and stretching routines to increase your muscle stamina.

Getting started with beginners
by Philippa Bunting

Beginners can't be wrong, only wrongly taught!

Teaching beginners is the biggest challenge there is. Every time a new pupil walks into the room, your teaching comes fundamentally into question. Perhaps not the core of your philosophy or basic principles of technical development (though we all meet individual students who force us, in the most positive sense, to revisit these) but all the detail: the when, the what, the how and, sometimes, even the why.

Beginners come in all shapes, sizes and ages, with all sorts of previous musical experience, but they all have one thing in common: this is the first time they've had a teacher focus on them and on helping them discover this instrument. And it's fun!

> The right time to start teaching is when the pupil wants to start. Or maybe just a little later...

Getting started

So your pupil has made the most important move: expressing an interest in learning. Another musical journey is about to start – what next?

First find out as much as you can about your new pupil:

- How old is s/he?
- Why does s/he want to learn this instrument?
- What musical experience does s/he have already?
- What else is s/he learning?
- Are there any Special Educational Needs that you need to take into account?
- In the case of some instruments, are there any physical factors that might affect the decision?

If the pupil is learning in a school/music centre environment you'll probably have to glean this from existing records, and as time goes on, directly from the pupil. If in a private context, grill the parents/carers! During the conversation, make clear your own expectations, including arrangements for payment, missed lessons and other practical details.

As with any project, clear planning will help everybody involved enjoy the experience more, and, hopefully, avoid any disasters or pitfalls along the way. Armed with the information you have gathered in your initial contact with pupil or parents/carers, time spent thinking through the following issues will considerably ease the initial stages:

- Individual or group lessons?
- Length of lesson?
- Role of parents/carers?
- Hiring or buying an instrument?

- Goals
- Resources and materials
- Activities and games
- Planning
- Teaching standard notation
- Motivation

Let's look at each of these in turn:

Individual or group lessons?

For most children, the ideal learning environment would be a combination of both individual and group work, with the individual work providing focus and the group-work reinforcement, learning from peers, ensemble skills and the all-important social element.

If you have control over the timetabling of your lessons, you might well consider bringing beginners of a similar age together for the first stages, then reviewing whether to continue as a group or work individually. If you have the luxury of two points of contact in a week then you could offer one individual and one group lesson, perhaps organising a cluster of individual lessons around a central group experience on the same day. In an ideal world, the more points of contact in a week you can achieve in the early stages, the better, on the principle of little and often.

> We learn as much, if not more, from those who are close to us in terms of experience, than from those who are already experts.

Length of lesson

It would be wise to leave this open until you meet the pupil in question and get a feel for their concentration span. It is vital to get the duration right so that each pupil leaves wanting more, but not feeling at all rushed. A tight, well-paced lesson focuses not only the pupil's mind but yours as well. As a rough rule of thumb for individual lessons, start a young child with 20 to 25 minutes and go up in increments of 5 minutes as the material you are using increases in length and complexity. For group lessons, start with 35 to 40 minutes and do likewise.

If you don't have control over this aspect, then consider doing what you can to maximise the time each pupil spends with you, even if this is at the expense of individual attention.

Role of parents/carers

It is vital to stress from the earliest stages that parents/carers need to be closely involved in the process of a child learning an instrument, and that it is they who will be doing the bulk of the work in the early stages. They don't need to bring any knowledge to the party, just a relaxed and appreciative interest – it may be useful to refer to 'playing at home' rather than 'practise' to reinforce this – and most importantly they need to ensure that the child plays every day, if possible for a series of short bursts rather than one long session. Getting them to write notes in lessons can be a great help.

If you are teaching in a situation where there is no direct contact with parents/carers, you might consider producing a set of guidance notes for them, detailing your expectations, your expectations of your pupil, and ideas to help parents/carers support a child's learning. Clear notes, either in a practice book or on the music itself, will be important, and you will have to be absolutely clear in your instructions since it is your pupil who will be taking responsibility for understanding what needs to be done at home. If you don't have the parent/carer in the lesson, consider calling them a few weeks into the term to tell them how well their child is doing.

> To most people, criticism always sounds *fortissimo*, and praise *pianissimo*. Remember to do what you can to adjust the volume!

Adult beginners
Clearly the adult beginner will be responsible for his/her own learning at home in the early stages, but this is pretty much the only difference to a child pupil. Repertoire, and the vocabulary you use, will need to be carefully chosen, but the essential principles hold true. All beginners are young in terms of their knowledge of the subject in hand, and adults in particular, with their well-developed sense of self-criticism, need constant reassurance and praise. Their worst fault, in my experience, is wanting to talk too much before getting down to the doing!

Hiring or buying an instrument
It is important to give clear guidance on buying or hiring an instrument to avoid the common situation where the pupil comes to the first lesson clutching something utterly inappropriate but in which s/he has already invested emotionally. Separating the child from an instrument with which s/he has bonded can make the first few weeks' work doubly hard.

For instruments where sizing is crucial, it is probably best to wait until the first meeting to advise on a suitable instrument, given how much children can grow in the course of a few months or so. If the instruments come from a central stock to which you have access then take as many as is practicable to the first lesson. If not, then finding the right one can be the goal for the first week, and personalising it by decorating the case and choosing accessories as one cares for it an on-going project. We all play better on an instrument we love and care for, which we feel belongs to us alone. The first step in building a beautiful tone is to develop a bond with the physical instrument itself, to make it a part of you.

Goals
Being clear about what you are aiming for, and celebrating achievement along the way, is particularly important with beginners. As players advance, the music becomes a motivation in itself, but it is a rare beginner who can derive that kind of self-motivation in the early stages. To borrow from the business world, targets for beginners need to be SMART – Specific, Measurable, Achievable, Relevant and Timed! For example:
- Perform a simple piece with accompaniment by the end of lesson one.
- Maintain a pulse whilst performing rhythms made up of crotchets and quavers, or crotchets and minims, by the end of lesson six.
- Prepare a short piece from memory for performance at an informal concert at the end of term.

Don't be afraid of setting very little work in the initial stages. As we all know, habits practised wrongly can be very hard to eradicate later, and you will be wanting to set up and reinforce really good habits in these early stages. On the other hand, it is also important you make sure your pupils have something ready to perform early on, and at all times throughout their learning. Informal performance opportunities are vital to artistic development – encourage them to play to anybody and everybody who'll listen!

Resources and materials

With the pupil and your goals firmly in mind, you can start to look at existing resources to see whether they fit your needs and those of your pupil. Go with an open mind to any existing methods available and ask the simple question – how can this help me and my pupils? The chances of you finding one that achieves an exact fit is small, but there is something to be learned from all of them. It can be convenient to have at least one central reference book as a focus for pupil, teacher and parent/carer, supplemented by your own material and that of others, published or unpublished.

Next comes the fun part! First, fill in the gaps you've identified in the methods and then, once the lessons start, develop material and resources to feed your pupil's own growing interests. The smaller the gap between the beginner and the resources you provide, the more personal they are, the better the result. Bring the experience to the child. Once they are confident in their own space, they will be able to enter into other musical spaces and experiences with increasing frequency and maturity.

> Don't be afraid to re-invent the wheel. The process of so doing can clarify things in your own mind, and help your development as a thinking, creative and flexible teacher.

Activities and games

With the resources and repertoire chosen, you now need to think about how you are going to work with your material. Instrumental teaching has traditionally focused very much on the visual aspect, on realising notes from a page. However, in order to get the most out of early lessons, this needs to be complemented by activities which involve aural and movement-based work. Casting anything as a game will create an atmosphere of creative play, and ensure sufficient repetition to fix whichever concept you are trying to communicate. Remember: playing is something people, particularly children, usually do willingly, and with joy!

Use a range of resources and materials of different textures and colours, and intersperse static activities with ones which involve moving. Actively encourage early forays into the world of improvisation and composition, with you learning and exploring alongside your pupils.

Planning

Planning is a vital aspect of teaching. Not the kind of planning that puts you in a straitjacket and prevents you from responding to the individual, but that which ensures you have all the right resources to hand, and that lessons have a focus and are well-paced. This is particularly true in the early stages, where there is so much to exchange that choices must be made and priorities set. Keep the following headings in mind as you plan, and the process will help you reach the right balance within a lesson or across a group of lessons:

- Posture and technical development
- Rhythm and pitch
- Notation
- Improvisation and composition
- Expression
- Sense of style and musical form
- Preparation for performance

If you can't fit everything into one lesson, don't worry. Just give it time in the next.

Teaching standard notation

The emphasis you place on note-reading is a matter for you to decide, and one which will vary according to the age and experience of your pupils as well as their preferred learning styles. This said, the ability to read is one which will stand any musician in good stead when playing with others, and in the majority of cases learning it in easily digestible stages as early as possible is probably the most sensible approach.

Start with the most basic concepts such as high/low, line/space, left/right and separate pitch from rhythm. Explore a range of possible shorthands, and consider adopting a set of syllables to represent pitches (such as relative *solfa*), or rhythm names (such as *ta, ti-ti*).

There are many ways of learning and making music which don't involve notation - after all, music is primarily a sound, not a sight. Try exploring some you're not yet familiar with, then share them with your pupils.

Motivation

Usually motivation, in terms of energy and interest, is high in the very early stages. It is important that this is reinforced for your pupil by successes which are concrete and celebrated. You may want to consider a system of rewards – though this can work against the kind of intrinsic motivation you are trying to foster.

Performances are an important motivator, and need to form part of all your pupils' experience. The more informal these are in the early stages, the better for confidence-building. Encourage pupils to introduce themselves and tell their audience a bit about the piece they are about to play, to encourage individuality in performance.

> Knowing how hard something is motivates only a few brave souls. Knowing how easy it is suits us lesser mortals better.

So here it is – the first lesson

Make sure you have the room prepared as you want it, and any resources and materials you plan to use easily to hand. If the pupil isn't bringing an instrument with them, you need a suitable one for them to play. Put a chair where you want the parent/carer to sit (behind the child and at a little distance from the area you plan to work in) and one for the child, if necessary.

When the pupil comes into the room, avoid any lengthy preambles, but go straight in with some practical activities. These need to be ones which enable you quickly to assess the child's previous musical experience (some simple copying games using clapping and singing for example) and also a physical warm-up, using movements they will need when playing.

> Try to use the word 'do' rather than 'don't' as much as possible.

It is important that the whole lesson is full of doing, and that you gear it towards an achievable performance at the end. The disappointment of going to a first lesson and not playing anything could provide a setback that takes valuable time to correct. Find ways to avoid explaining a vast number of things before you embark on activities, remembering that doing is the most direct way of learning, and that the thinking and full understanding will come with time and repeated experience. Try also to avoid too many discrete activities as these will interrupt the flow of the experience for the pupil.

Use elements from the piece you are aiming for throughout the lesson, so that they are familiar before the pupil comes to the final performance. For example:

- Establish the bar time with some physical movements.
- Rehearse any movements needed for playing away from the instrument.
- If the rhythm is very simple, introduce some clapping exercises based on the accompaniment so that it will be familiar when heard.
- Teach a song which contains the same rhythm or pitch relationships as those in the target piece.
- Contextualise the piece by exploring its title, or giving it words.
- If there are rests in the piece, introduce activities supportive of good playing posture to be performed in them.

> Incorporating a wide range of activities, including movement and copying, will help you cater for the full range of preferred learning styles amongst your pupils.

At the end of the lesson, set clear targets for work at home, and refer to what you will be doing in the next lesson. Praise everything the pupil has achieved, and be positive about the musical journey to come. Research has shown that a loving relationship with one's first teacher is one of the two most important predictors of future success in music.

The other is sheer volume of practice!

Philippa Bunting
MA, Assistant Director (Academic),
Royal Northern College of Music

Further reading

Children's Minds M. Donaldson (HarperCollins ISBN 0006861229)

The Developmental Psychology of Music D. Hargreaves (CUP ISBN 0521314151)

How Children Fail J. Holt (Penguin Books Ltd. ISBN 0140135561)

How Children Learn J. Holt (Penguin Books Ltd. ISBN 0140136002)

Group teaching

by Nick Beach

*Group teaching is not an economic necessity, not a compromise and not a
second class learning experience. In fact, group teaching is the best way
for most children to learn a musical instrument. In this chapter I will look
at what needs to be in place for group teaching to be successful and some
ways around common problems.*

Ask any adult who had instrumental lessons as a child what their most
positive musical experiences were and the answer will probably revolve
around the experience of music as a group activity. If you ask the opposite
question regarding negative musical experience and the overwhelming
majority of people will refer to their instrumental lesson, almost always an
individual one.

Now let's look at a specific group of people: instrumental music teachers.
This group was successful in their instrumental playing at school and many
went to university or conservatoire to study music. While this group was at
school they were the instrumental high-flyers. Individual attention for them
was a godsend – it allowed them to get all that they needed from their
teacher. Ask them as adults about their relationship with their teacher and
the majority will speak of a debt of gratitude they feel for everything that the
teacher did for them.

Considering these different experiences illustrates why, as instrumental
teachers, many of us are reluctant to embrace group teaching: because it
would not have suited us. Let's face it, high-flying pupils create a problem
in a group teaching context. It's a great problem to have and one which we
all look forward to having, but it is a problem nonetheless. Of course we
should have high aspirations for all our pupils but the vast majority of them
are not going to go on to study music. We teach musical instruments because
we believe that music provides a life-enriching experience for the pupil – not
because every now and then we will have a high-flyer who goes to a
conservatoire. We need to look for the best ways for pupils to access that life-
enriching musical experience and for the huge majority of pupils it is best
delivered in a group context.

Group teaching – individual learning

Many of the problems associated with group teaching stem from semantics.
If we had never invented the label 'group instrumental teaching' but instead
had referred to 'class instrumental teaching' there would be a much better
understanding of what we are trying to do. A group is defined as 'a number
of individuals joined together', whereas a class is a single entity which can
be broken down into constituent parts.

Translated into teaching activity, the group teacher is struggling to
give a number of concurrent individual lessons, whilst the class
teacher is giving one lesson that allows for the individual needs of
all members of the class.

The most successful group teachers draw on many of the techniques of the classroom teacher: effective management of space, planning and record-keeping, being in four places at once, and so on!

> The key to successful group teaching is 'all involved, all the time'.

But what about technique?

A secure technique is one of the foundations upon which an enriching musical experience is built. Many of us had individual lessons where the basis of our secure technique was founded. Individual teaching encourages a particular style of teaching which does not transfer easily into the group context. This has led some teachers to say that you cannot teach technique effectively in a group lesson.

Of course the individual diagnostic approach to technical development will not work in a group lesson – it would end up as a series of short and unsatisfactory individual lessons. What is required is a class approach to the teaching of technique which is no less rigorous but does not focus on individual correction.

Teaching technique to the class
Many string players learn good bowing style with a teacher who physically guides their movements. This cannot be done in a group lesson – but the following is just as effective:
1. Identify the movements involved in a good bowing style and try them without using the bow.
2. Use sticks instead of bows and 'shadow bow' with the stick resting on the shoulder.
3. The group does this miming to music which you play.
4. Transfer these movements to the real bow on open strings.

Children are experts at working in a group context
Children work every day in a group context in the classroom. Some children relish the unique environment that is provided by an individual lesson, but it is important to realise just how unique this individualised experience is for the child. For most, this individual lesson will be the longest time they spend with any adult other than their parents/carers in their normal week.

Children working in a group context are not only likely to be more relaxed and comfortable, but they are also likely to have more fun! The group situation allows for a whole range of games and other activities which help them understand the joy of music-making.

Notation
Lay out a large stave on the floor using string or tape. Then use the children themselves as noteheads. There are plenty of activities here: they can sing or play the notes they are standing on, they can arrange themselves in a pattern you have played or one of the group can play a pattern the rest are forming.

Pulse
Take some balls into the lesson. The children work in pairs and bounce the ball to each other, bouncing on one beat and catching on the next. When they can do this well they can sing their pieces at the same time as bouncing the ball.

If the group is well managed it also has access to a support structure which not only gives help when one member is struggling but also celebrates their successes.

> *I am reminded of a group in which I had a child with severe physical difficulties. Now the instant reaction might have been to arrange individual lessons for this child but to do so would have given in to the problems he faced. His physical problems meant that he was always going to struggle with the technical aspects of playing the violin but with the support of the group he achieved far beyond what he (or anyone else) expected, with all the benefits for his general education that this promoted. His successes were celebrated by the rest of the group and his feeling of achievement was wonderful to share in.*

Taking control of the space

Planning the space

How many stories have we heard of music lessons being sidelined to broom cupboards, cricket pavilions, offices, and so on? The disgrace is that this does happen and at the heart of each story is a group of children who have had their educational experience diminished by the environment in which they are expected to learn.

To some extent we have brought this upon ourselves. We are passionate about bringing musical experiences to our pupils and rather than saying 'No, this space is not good enough for pupils to learn in' we have said 'Well, it's not ideal but we'll muddle through until something better becomes available.' Often it does not; once the headteacher realises that s/he can get away with asking you to teach in that corridor/sick room you are there forever. We do not all have the luxury of being able to say no, but it is important to understand that the environment in which children learn is fundamental to their learning experience.

What sort of space do we need for group teaching and how should we organise it?

The second question here is a vital one as many group lessons take place in a space which could be perfectly acceptable given a bit of organisation. The minimum space needed for a group lesson is one where each member of the group can have their own music stand and there is enough space for the teacher to get around the group in all directions. It is absolutely vital that young learners do not feel restricted when playing – that way lies all sorts of technical problems. The essence of technique on any instrument concerns freedom of movement and nothing inhibits that freedom more than the fear of bumping against someone else, the wall or the furniture.

But what about the peripatetic/itinerant teacher – how can they make the best of what they are given? We are always pressed for time but there is no substitute for moving stuff out of the way to create a good space for playing in. Often this will mean moving tables, shifting the chairs in the staff room, or otherwise ensuring that the learning environment is as good as possible. An instrumental lesson crammed into the corner of a classroom full of tables engenders a feeling of 'not belonging' and impermanence. Often a few tables moved to the side can make a space in which real learning can take place.

Serried ranks or chamber music?

How might we arrange the group to help the learning process? Personally, I prefer the semi-circle arrangement with the teacher at the centre of the circle. In this arrangement the main focus of the pupils is on you as the teacher, but also they can see one another.

I don't think the teacher should use a music stand as they should know what they are teaching – if you need to check something you can glance at a pupil's music. If you do use one it should be set really low and nowhere near the sight lines between you and the pupils.

The semi-circle arrangement also allows you to get around behind the group from time to time, but I think it is un-nerving for the pupils to have the whole lesson conducted from behind them.

Music stands: a necessary evil!

The music stand's only positive attribute is that it props up the music! Everything else about it is detrimental to the lesson: it is a barrier between pupils and teacher, it takes up valuable space, it is unstable and most children seem to be able to make a range of sculptures when folding one away that makes the origami flapping bird seem easy!

I suggest keeping music stands out of the way for every part of the lesson where they are not essential. For the same reason that great string quartets play from memory, the level of communication between teacher and pupils when the stands are out of the way is greatly enhanced. If you are adopting the semi-circle approach outlined above it is a simple matter for the pupils to get into the habit of putting the stands out of the way behind them when they are not being used.

Teaching strategies

Using your instrument

Why is it that, as teachers, we feel we have to teach so much? We have this almost pathological drive to tell people how to do things, to explain, to elaborate. And in the corner of the room (or boot of the car) in a box is the tool which can provide instant enlightenment and sweep away a myriad of explanations – our instrument!

Children are genetically driven to copy adults – this is how they learn from the earliest stages of their development. No one explains pronunciation to a young child – they just demonstrate. There are huge problems with verbal explanations, not least that they favour a particular learning style. A child cannot truly understand a point of technique until they have experienced it, and no amount of verbal explanation will replace that experience. If the quickest way to achieve this is to say 'copy me' – then do it!

Structure

This is the heart of the matter. Without a reliable structure to the lesson, group instrumental teaching can turn into a rather unfocused mess of individual activity, individual inactivity and haphazard group work.

It is important to understand what we mean by structure – we do not mean a minute-by-minute rigid plan for the lesson which the teacher will stick to come what may. We mean a framework within which fits the planned activities for the lesson and which provides the pupils with a clear and logical approach. Pupils enjoy the security that this structured approach gives them and look forward to the various elements of the lesson – especially if there are regular 'fun' activities to anticipate.

An effective medium-term plan allows the teacher to concentrate on limited areas of development in the lesson, safe in the knowledge that everything is covered by 'the plan'.

Sample lesson structure for four players

Here is a typical structure for a group of four players, all playing different pieces:

Warm-up section

> The warm-up section will introduce the aim(s) of the lesson and all four players will be using the same material. The teacher employs a variety of strategies, exercises and games which give each pupil the chance to operate below, at, and above their level. Some activities may function at multiple levels of course.

Body of the lesson

> There are three main strategies group teachers use when pupils are playing different pieces. The strategy used will depend on the aims for the lesson.
>
> 1. **Extract:** take an extract from one pupil's piece and use this as the focus of the lesson with the whole group.
> 2. **Perform:** one pupil performs their piece and it is reviewed by the group and the teacher.
> 3. **Accompany:** ostinatos or accompanying parts of appropriate standard are provided by the teacher for use by the other pupils.

Review

> Reinforcing the most significant parts of the lesson for each pupil.

Here are two sample situations:

Sample lesson plan: group 1

Group 1 is five instrumentalists who have been learning for two terms.
The aim of the lesson is the technical, musical and reading implications of dynamics.

Warm-up
- Call and response: clapping loud and soft patterns, relating volume changes to energy level.
- Call and response on instruments: making loud and soft sounds.

Body of the lesson (everyone playing the same piece)
- Play through the piece together.
- Individuals play a phrase at different volumes: discuss the effect.
- Decide on a dynamics plan for the piece: discuss it and try it out.
- One pupil 'conducts' the others, directing the volume.
- What does the music tell us: are there other dynamics we want to add?

Summary
- How do we make dynamic changes?
- How are they written in the music?
- What changes do they make to the mood?

Group 2 is three instrumentalists who are preparing to take Grade 2 in a term's time. One of them is struggling with the pieces and falling behind. The aim of the lesson is to develop confidence in playing the more difficult piece and improve practice technique.

Planning
- Select a hard bit from the piece and divide it into fragments.

Warm-up
- Start with call and response on very easy patterns.
- Very gradually (almost imperceptibly) steer the fragments towards the shape of the hard bit.
- Gradually construct the hard bit from the fragments.
- Before they know it they will be playing the hard bit!

Body of the lesson
- Now play the hard bit from the music. Look at it in context: play the phrase it comes from together.
- Go to an easier section and select a single phrase which each pupil plays in turn. The group discusses how each could improve.
- Discuss how the music will need to sound to get a distinction, and what is needed to get there.

Summary
- The group discusses a 'practice plan' for each of their personal tricky bits. The target is to sort them out by next week.

Some other issues

Mixed ability teaching

This is probably the thorniest area of the group teaching debate: teachers vary widely on the breadth of standard they are prepared to accommodate within their groups. This makes it very hard to define exactly what we mean by mixed ability teaching. Whatever the approach to this issue, the key to successful group teaching – all involved, all the time – still applies.

Let's go back to our group of four players playing different pieces (page 37). There is a lot of different music to get through: the answer is to focus on the aims of the lesson, whether those aims are to do with developing technical ability, gaining knowledge or fostering an emotional understanding of the music, or, of course, a combination. The aim of the lesson should not be to play all the way through all the pieces that the pupils have prepared.

Let's assume that our group is clarinettists and the aim is to develop their ability to cross over the break. For some pupils this may be a preparatory activity – they have not done it yet. For others it could be a developmental activity – they are learning to do it better. For the rest it might be a reviewing activity – they do it well already but are reinforcing their skills. It is irrelevant to none of them.

At the heart of any lesson is the musical experience for the pupils, and as long as this remains the first priority then there is no reason why pupils should not be taught in mixed ability groups. However, it does require more preparation from the teacher to ensure they are prepared with resources for every eventuality.

The ensemble music route

Having a number of young musicians in the room at the same time widens the range of repertoire that teachers can draw upon. However, there are some dangers in going too far along the chamber music route.

Firstly, it is important to remember that this is a lesson, not a rehearsal. Whilst much useful work can be done in the 'coaching' environment, the tendency will be to give the playing of the notes and aspects of ensemble priority over technical and musical development.

The second pitfall is that, because each of the players is playing something different, this will turn into a series of individual lessons, concentrating in turn on the difficulty each player faces. Such a lesson can quickly loose sight of our 'all involved all the time' maxim. This is not to say that there is no place for chamber music in the lesson but remember that successful group teaching must have a balance of activities.

Having fun

The group lesson provides an instant resource for having a good time making music – whether through games, chamber music, performance to each other, or even as an audience for your terrible jokes! As instrumental teachers we are lucky: the children don't have to learn an instrument. If they are not enjoying themselves, feeling a sense of achievement and feeling appropriately challenged they will give up.

Children will only learn when the three criteria of **enjoyment**, **challenge** and **achievement** are being met. As teachers, we have to give these three areas absolute priority. It is a rare case of educational priority matching with funding necessity.

Sharing the load

Teaching instrumental/vocal music in groups is hard work. There are times when we struggle to keep that enthusiasm going and feel short of ideas. It is vital to have some kind of support network, whether a formal one provided by teachers from the same organisation, or a less formal network of like-minded teachers. Whatever the structure, sharing ideas, problems and resources will benefit you and your colleagues enormously.

And finally . . .

The capacity of children to learn is limited only by the opportunities we provide for that learning to take place. Education systems, by their very nature, put as many barriers in the way of children's learning as they provide openings. Within the context of instrumental tuition we have a unique opportunity to explore: to push the boundaries of traditional wisdom, to try new things, and find new ways of unlocking the potential within each child.

Ten top tips for successful group teaching

- Teach the class, not the individuals.

- Aim to talk less and demonstrate more.

- Take control of the space.

- Try to loose the music stands sometimes.

- Plan well and keep good records.

- The warm-up is a key element of the lesson.

- The review is also a key element of the lesson!

- Children only learn when they are enjoying themselves.

- Share the load.

- Experiment, experiment, experiment!

Nick Beach
Deputy Director,
Trinity Guildhall
Examinations

Teaching pupils with a learning disability *by Rosie Cross*

Ziekel is eight years old, plays the piano with enthusiasm and has Down syndrome. His grandmother told me that there had been a case conference at his mainstream school involving his teachers, support workers and parents, and that comments had been made about how beneficial Ziekel's piano playing had been in terms of motor co-ordination, speech, general learning, self-confidence and self-expression. As Ziekel's piano teacher, I wish I had been invited. I am, after all, in the privileged position of working with him on a one-to-one basis every week.

Ziekel is lucky. Most children with a learning disability (LD) such as Down syndrome, autistic spectrum disorder or dyslexia do not have the chance to play, in spite of the enormous benefits that can result, because there are not enough teachers willing to take them on. This situation must change.

General advice for teachers

Successful teaching must be a partnership between parent/carer and teacher. The parent/carer must ensure that the teacher knows about the child and his particular disabilities as well as what he is like as a person: his likes and dislikes, and the way he responds to changing situations. It is recommended that, before lessons start, a frank meeting takes place between the teacher and parent or carer.

- Both parties must be open about their aims for the future and discuss how they hope to work together, and both must be open about their reservations and fears.
- The parent/carer must not be afraid to say when it is clear that a certain activity will not work, so that alternatives can be discussed.
- The teacher must take every opportunity to get to know the child as a person and must therefore consider the relationship with the parent to be an essential part of that process.
- Parents/carers are usually keen that their child should be treated just like all the others and may not be forthcoming about the disability (often parents/carers are in denial themselves regarding the disability).
- Teachers are experts in their field – parents/carers and carers therefore look to them for guidance – but music teachers are not experts in learning disabilities. In fact, parents/carers are the experts when it comes to knowing their own child. A good working partnership will lead to rewards and benefits for all, not only in music but in many other areas.
- Be open about the fact that it may be your first pupil with a LD; generally parents/carers are very supportive and grateful for the opportunity. You will find the experience both rewarding and exciting.

> Establish a relationship with parents/carers and pupil, and begin a journey of exploration.

Nicholas Chisholme, Headmaster of the Yehudi Menuhin School, when talking about the educational needs of the exceptionally gifted (EG), said that rather than seeing the ability range as a straight line, he prefers to see it as a circle where the educational needs of a child with LD are very similar to those who are exceptionally gifted in a particular area such as music. The task is to discover and assess a pupil's ability and potential and enable them to achieve it.

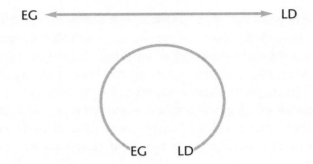

The most common learning difficulties

The main LDs encountered are Down syndrome, autistic spectrum disorder (which includes Asperger's Syndrome) and dyslexia. Here are some brief characteristics, but teachers are advised to make their own investigations.

Down syndrome (caused by an extra chromosome)
- Poor muscle tone.
- Poor co-ordination.
- Low IQ.
- Possible health problems involving heart and hearing which may affect the choice of instrument.

Autistic spectrum disorder (cause unknown)
- Difficulties with interaction with the world practically and socially.
- Can be exceptionally gifted in one area, but unable to live independently.

Dyslexia (there is often a family history of dyslexia)
- Often characterised by difficulties with writing and reading, in spite of a high IQ. Most examining boards allow extra time for dyslexic pupils.
- May well be lacking in confidence.

> Within each category of learning disability there is a variety of personalities and abilities. Each child is different.

Choosing an instrument

Keyboard/piano
- Ideal because of the visual quality: the notes are laid out in front of the pupil.
- Little physical effort is required.
- There are no tuning or intonation problems.

Strings

- These instruments require a good ear for pitch.
- Little physical effort is required, although some stamina is required to hold up a violin.

Brass and woodwind

- These instruments require physical strength to blow: pupils with a LD are advised to seek medical advice before taking up one of these instruments.

Recorder

- A good instrument to try before embarking on woodwind or brass.
- Not expensive.
- Pupils with Down syndrome tend to have short but wide fingers so may be better off with a treble or tenor recorder.

Percussion and drum kit

- For a pupil with a good sense of rhythm, this may be ideal.

General dos and don'ts

DO

- Accept slow progress.
- Accept lessons that achieve nothing.
- Accept failure and have the confidence to change your mind if something doesn't work.
- Question each activity: for example, is reading notation appropriate for this child?
- Examine and question your methodology.
- Have plenty of material prepared, and be ready to change activity frequently during a lesson.
- Be firm, predictable and consistent.
- If you promise something, keep to it. People with a LD don't always understand changed circumstances and can feel betrayed.
- Encourage positive feelings in parents/carers. They are probably just as worried about failure as you are.

DO NOT

- Change the routine. If you do, explain very carefully first what is going to happen.
- Change the time, furniture, etc, especially with a child with one of the ASD problems: their security and link with the outside world often rests in familiarity of surroundings and activity.
- Be impatient to see progress. It will often be spasmodic.
- Ask a pupil to do something unless you are confident that he can do it. If in doubt, discuss with the parent first.
- Feel guilty that you have been paid to teach this lesson and have little to show for it.

How to begin

There are three main areas of progress; your activities should seek to develop all three:

1. Develop muscle tone, strong hands and agile fingers.
2. Increase the repertoire of music that can be played.
3. Develop improvisation.

Pupils with poor co-ordination will find it easier to use the middle three fingers of each hand first. This seems to be particularly true of those with Down syndrome. Start with these fingers: *Merrily we roll along* or *Mary had a little lamb* work well on three black notes on the piano, or B A G on the flute, clarinet or recorder. *Twinkle, twinkle, little star* works well and can be learned by rote fairly easily. There are numerous examples, together with many five finger exercises.

People with a LD like repetition and familiarity and often enjoy scales and exercises. Establish a routine whereby you always start a lesson with this sort of work to improve muscle tone, and you may find your pupils won't want to play anything at all until they have been through their scales and exercises!

> My pupil with Down syndrome, who ten years ago had difficulty playing the three black notes on the piano because his muscle tone was so poor, now begins each lesson with all the white major and minor scales, hands together, one octave. He loves them.

Some pupils with a LD can be stubborn and difficult: don't let this affect your relationship with them. Be firm, be consistent, be predictable.

Which tutor to use

There are many tutors available for pupils of all ages, and much well presented and attractive music. It is a good idea to use a tutor book, so that progress can be seen to be taking place, even if you have many digressions from it, and teach the contents by rote. Award stickers when a piece has been achieved, whether by rote or by reading or by a mixture of both. Be firm: no going on to the next piece until the previous one is finished. I recommend the Alfred series for the very young beginner on the piano, because they progress very slowly and have a lot of material in a five-finger position, even before the stave is introduced. Don't follow a set method that has been successful with other pupils without checking whether it will be appropriate for this pupil.

If someone does not read words easily, it would be foolish to expect him to read notation. This would be an activity that detracts from rather than supports the playing of the instrument. It is possible to find ways of playing without reading notation.

The importance of improvisation

I believe that for those with a LD, the key to successful playing on any instrument lies in improvisation. It encourages free creative expression; it does not depend on written notation; it can be adapted to suit a pupil of any ability and allows the pupil to take charge of his own learning as you develop this type of playing together. Some very simple examples for a beginner could be:

Happy and sad. Draw two faces on a piece of paper and ask the pupil to tell you on their instrument which one s/he is thinking about. This can then be discussed, and contrasts of loud and soft, fast and slow can be explored.

Storm, with thunder and lightning. This can be used to explore loud and soft playing and high and low pitch. Raindrops can give an excellent opportunity to work on the need to play *staccato*.

Here are two more advanced examples of improvisations that have been developed on the piano by my pupils. Their work was supported by a parent or carer who attended the lessons and gave help during the week.

Sailing

Sailing was created by Ziekel, aged eight, as a development of the piece called *Sailing* in the Alfred Lesson book A. It explores the contrasts of high and low pitches, fast and slow speeds and loud and soft. It also introduces the idea of hand crossing on the keyboard. The pianist illustrates the story on the keyboard as the storyteller (parent or carer) tells the story.

The story	The music
It was a lovely, hot sunny day when Ziekel went sailing on the sea.	Put both hands on the keyboard and use all the fingers to produce a slow and gentle swaying movement.
Some seagulls were flying in the sky.	Improvise at the top end of the piano then resume the swaying motion.
One seagull flew down and stole Ziekel's sandwich right out of his hand.	A finger **glissando** down the keyboard, a sharp tap on a cluster of notes followed by a **glissando** up again.
A friendly dolphin was swimming in the sea.	Improvise at the low end of the keyboard and then resume the swaying motion.
The dolphin liked to jump right over Ziekel's boat.	The left hand improvises some dolphin music at the bottom of the keyboard, crosses over the right hand and plays a high note cluster and then moves back to the dolphin music at the bottom.
(The dolphin sequence can be repeated more than once.)	
At the end of a lovely day, Ziekel said goodbye to the seagulls that were flying in the sky.	Resume the swaying music, followed by the seagull music at the top of the keyboard.
He said goodbye to the dolphin who was swimming in the sea...	Resume the swaying music and then play one last dolphin jump.
...and Ziekel sailed home.	The music gets quieter and slower.

All in a day's work

The inspiration for this extended improvisation was Grieg's *Morning*. My pupil, Tom, heard and enjoyed this melody and wanted to play it himself. He had been having piano lessons for nine years. The resulting programme takes between two and three minutes to play, but the work involved in achieving this took several months to prepare.

Learning objectives

Listening
Reading music or rote learning

Playing duets
Ensemble playing
Preparation

Quiet playing
Creative improvisation

Creative improvisation
Appreciation of melody and accompaniment

Preparation of the Morning sequence

I taught Tom to play the melody of **Morning** with his right hand by rote, as he does not read music. This could also be done by using the letter names of the notes, or by reading notation.

As an accompaniment to the melody, I wanted Tom to add in some chords in the left hand. To teach him about chords, we learned a simple C major tune. We played it together, with him playing the following chord pattern at the bottom of the piano while I played the tune above.

Then Tom and I talked about what comes before morning: the quiet of the night. We experimented with playing quietly, to suggest the stillness that comes before morning. Then we remembered the dawn chorus, the singing and twittering of the birds, which we created on the high notes of the piano.

The Morning sequence
We now had a **Morning** sequence:
- A description of the stillness of the night, leading into early morning, played with both hands in the two octaves from middle C upwards on the piano.
- The dawn chorus, played at the top of the piano.
- Grieg's **Morning**, accompanied by C, F and G⁷ chords in the left hand:

At this point during a lesson an ice cream van drove by, playing ***Whistle while you work***. This tune appealed to Tom, and we decided we could add it to our ***Morning*** sequence, to suggest people getting up and going off to work. He learned this tune by rote, but as with ***Morning***, you could teach it by using letter names or notation.

Listening
Reading/Rote learning
Preparation

We then experimented with sounds to suggest the working day: a police car, fire engine, bulldozer, typewriter, etc. I thought ***Intercity stomp**** by Chris Norton would be a suitable tune to learn to add to our work sounds. Rote teaching of this proved to be too difficult, but we did manage three extracts from it.

Listening
Reading/Rote learning
Changes in dynamics

Based on ***Intercity stomp***, we did a lot of improvised duet work, with responsive copying of ideas between two pianists.

Concentrated listening
Responsive playing
Ensemble work

Following on from our ***Morning*** sequence, we now had an extension to our programme:

- Extracts from ***Whistle while you work*** and ***Intercity stomp***, combined with improvised descriptions of the working day.
- This grows quieter, suggesting the end of the day, and leading into an evening tune and an improvisation around it. For example, ***Twinkle twinkle***, or a simple lullaby, with chord accompaniment.

Creative improvisation
Appreciation of melody and accompaniment

General learning objectives

As well as the particular learning objectives listed, there are a number of objectives that apply to playing in general:

- Playing with strong, agile fingers.
- Awareness and execution of dynamics.
- Access to a formal tune by means of rote learning or notation.
- Creative improvisation: developing the use of imagination in musical terms.
- Appreciation of melody and accompaniment and use of chords.
- Description of contrasting moods in pianistic terms.
- Duet and ensemble work – give and take on the keyboard in an improvisatory way.
- The ability to work on a programme and reproduce it over a period of weeks.

The benefits of working in this way spill over into –

1. *Language development*: discussing ideas and planning.
2. *Concentration*: remembering a fairly long programme.
3. *Motor co-ordination*: using individual finger work in a variety of ways: fast and slow, loud and soft, balancing melody and accompaniment.
4. *Personal development* and self-confidence.

Rosie Cross
GBSM, ARCM, ABSM,
PGCE, CTABRSM
Piano teacher

© 2005 by Rosie Cross

* Intercity Stomp comes from Microjazz Collection 2 by Christopher Norton, Boosey & Hawkes Music Publishers Ltd.

Further information

Melody: www.melody.me.uk

Melody has been set up to bring the pleasure and benefits of playing a musical instrument to people with a LD. There is a well-defined need to pool this expertise and share experience in this area. This is done through the Melody website and by holding training and discussion events for teachers and parents/carers. There is information on the website as well as links to relevant articles and ideas for improvisation.

British Dyslexia Association: www.bda-dyslexia.org.uk

National Music and Disability Information: info@soundsense.org

National Down Syndrome Society: www.ndss.org
www.nas.com: for a list of Down syndrome societies worldwide

The National Autistic Society: www.nas.org

British Institute of Learning Disabilities: www.bild.org.uk

Downs Educational Trust: www.downsed.org

Further reading

Understanding and working with the spectrum of autism Wendy Lawson
(Jessica Kingsley ISBN 1 85362 911 4) www.mugsy.org

The Practice Revolution: Getting great results from the six days between music lessons
Philip Johnson (Practicespot Press ISBN 0 9581905 0 X) www.practicespot.com

Coaching more advanced players *by Simon Young*

'Don't blame your hands; it's not their fault!'

After my time at the Paris Conservatoire I studied with Nadia Boulanger and she said this to me very early on in our relationship. My hands were only doing what I had told them, based on my limited knowledge (I needed to be made aware of the fact!) of the piece I was trying to play. She went on to make it clear to me that if there is something lacking in the playing the fault is either in the brain or the ear, or both. Later on, another teacher of mine, Cyril Smith, who had infinite patience while encouraging me to work out solutions for myself, reinforced this idea. Both these teachers also placed great emphasis on being able to sing phrases correctly, to study the score away from the instrument and to be able to play a piece in any key. Cyril used to say that you should aim to be 'perfect plus a margin'.

There are countless more gems like this that could fill a whole book, but what follows is the product not only of their teaching, but also of other teachers and musicians I have encountered as well as some of the not so good teaching that has come my way as a working musician over the last 30 years.

I am aware that not all of your students will be budding stars, but that should not stop you giving the best advice to and encouraging everyone with exactly the same amount of care and attention you would give to a very talented student. (I use the word student to indicate someone who studies with you and not necessarily someone who is at a university or conservatoire.)

Communicating, learning and enabling

Advanced students are at a stage when they need to become more autonomous and independent, and to help this process, teachers need to encourage more dialogue and discussion. Teaching is about communicating, learning is about connecting and practice is about enabling. Bad teaching does not communicate anything; the student does not connect, and ends up doing mindlessly repetitive practice to no meaningful end. The latter is to be avoided, always, but especially with advanced students as they are at a stage when they should understand why they are practising. As time becomes more precious good habits are essential for efficient and timesaving practice. Three of the most important aspects which should be developed during teaching and while practising are:
• good memory
• good inner ear
• good posture
All three are inextricably linked.

Good memory

Good memory needs the necessary time and attention in the first place otherwise the result is faulty recall of information inaccurately remembered. Mental rehearsal therefore is extremely important. Not just remembering the notes, but all the composer's instructions, personal interpretation (more of which later), and even the physical moves and correct fingering.

- Ask your student to look at the music and take in all the information they can about a specific phrase, including the way it should sound. When they are confident they have digested the information ask them to play it silently in their head using correct fingers, seeing themselves doing it in their mind's eye and hearing inwardly the end result.

- They may not be able to do this at the first attempt, but keep going until they can do this reasonably easily. Once they can do this ask them to play the phrase – they will immediately know when what they are doing is what they intend. In order to become proficient at this, students will need to develop their inner ear.

Inner ear

I have always found that the best way to develop the inner ear is to remove the other senses from the process. In its simplest form, closing one's eyes when listening helps the concentration enormously and can assist in developing instant recall. Sight-singing aloud and testing oneself before repeating the process silently is also helpful. Constantly testing interval recall and chord knowledge is essential. When the tonal spectrum has become instilled one can move to more contemporary harmonies with similar exercises.

Posture

Many problems are the result of incorrect posture which in turn can produce physical tension that is often difficult to remove. The forces at play here: tension, relaxation and effort, all need to interact while playing and it is therefore very important to balance these if correct posture is to be achieved.

Advanced students may come to you with bad habits and however success-fully you may achieve change in the lesson, under stress there is the strongest possibility that they will revert to habitual practice.
- The quickest way to make a student tense is to tell them to relax, so you will do well to find other strategies to help students to relax than to talk about it.
- One way is to get the student to focus on sound and the best means of achieving the most appropriate sound physically. Encourage them to investigate different possibilities, to breathe properly and to know why some movements produce better results than others.

It is possible to over-practise. It is a common fact that students will reach a plateau when studying a piece, a point at which they seem to be standing still. This is generally nothing to be worried about and simply means that the subconscious needs time to digest before moving on to the next stage of development. At this point a piece studied for a long time will benefit from a break before returning for further practice. This may happen more than once during the learning process; indeed it should be allowed to happen as many times as is necessary. This is best exemplified by the fact that whether performers return to a piece ten, twenty or a hundred times, they always find they learn something new and develop greater insight.

Choosing and explaining the right repertoire

Choosing the right repertoire can greatly assist the speed of a student's progress. I remember once being worried that a particular piece would be too difficult for a student, but having been persuaded to allow him to learn it, his technique moved very quickly onto a higher level.

- Present your choice enthusiastically. I often find that if I get excited about a contemporary piece the student wants to try it!
- Avoid simply lurching from one grade exam to the next, have valid reasons (see the section below on assessment).
- Encourage curiosity on the part of your students; they may come up with good ideas. My own repertoire has increased with pieces suggested by my students.
- Choose your response carefully when a student would like to play a piece that is technically beyond them. Discouraging them without care can put them against you.
- Build a repertoire that increases the student's knowledge.

Programming

Most artists find programming a fascinating subject and spend a great deal of time putting programmes together. Here are my top tips which can be applied to most occasions.

- Programmes should not be too long, shorter is always better.
- If there is a work that is difficult to listen to it should be balanced with something easy to listen to.
- Programmes that have a subject theme can often produce successful results.
- Composer's centenaries often provide useful ideas.
- Programmes of works by a single composer can be off-putting if not carefully thought through.
- If you know the acoustics of the hall in which your student will be playing it will help your choice of programme. The sound may be very dry, therefore pieces with thick textures would work well. If it is very resonant then the reverse would apply. There is nothing worse than having the extra pressure of doing something new to obtain clarity. However, it should also be an important part of your job to prepare advanced students for these eventualities!
- Always try to produce a balanced programme of style and interest.
- 'Interesting' is more important than 'difficult'.

An archetypal programme (without specifying instrument) might look something like the one on the left (below), but it could also look like the one on the right: do not be afraid to be inventive! These are, of course, examples for full recitals, but it is perfectly possible to create much smaller programmes using the same criteria. As a starting point you may wish to use only one of the four groups within the two boxes, but there are many permutations and nothing to stop you using only two or three pieces (or more) of the same genre where variety can be found.

Prelude (Baroque) Sonata (Classical) Romantic work Impressionist work Contemporary work	Prelude (Contemporary) Sonata (Romantic) Sonata (Baroque) Large Romantic work

Interpretation

Knowing a piece well gives one the confidence to see and feel beyond the notes: an essential element in the communication process. Successfully communicating the composer's intentions should be the aim of every student. Therefore:

- Encourage your student to base any interpretation upon all the facts at his disposal: the composer's markings and historical documentation as well as his own response to the music.
- Always discuss your reasons for any interpretative suggestions you may make. A teacher of mine once told me that it was not my place to make these kinds of decisions; I should do what I was told!
- Encourage listening to different recordings only after your student has the notes securely learnt. Listening too soon can create confusion and inhibit creativity.
- Have your student build in his interpretation from the moment he begins to study a piece, at this level this is crucial. Interpretation should not be something that is added at a later date once the notes have been leant. It should be part of the study from the very first note: how that note fits into the phrase, how the phrase fits into the structure and so on. Here I repeat the message of my very first paragraph, that the fingers can only make musical sense if the instruction is clear.

Teaching advanced adults

Advanced adults are difficult to teach for a number of reasons. They are probably the most set in their ways and may have good reason to mistrust you, especially if they have had a bad experience elsewhere. You will need all your wits about you to get the best results.

I will give you three examples of my own experience and leave you to draw your own conclusions.

Adult 1   A retired senior civil servant who wished he had applied to study at a conservatoire when he was a teenager.

Adult 2   A housewife whose children have all left the fold and who wishes to become proficient enough to begin a music therapy course.

Adult 3   A rich businessman and landowner who is passionate about playing and now has the time to devote to it.

Adult 1 had played all his life (without lessons most of the time) and had always regretted not taking the opportunity when young to study to become a professional musician. Thus he arrived for lessons with high expectations. He was by no means lacking in ability and had considerable facility, but had developed a large number of bad habits that it would be almost impossible to eradicate and it was patently obvious that he was completely unaware of this.

How does one approach this kind of task? It would be very easy to dismiss this person and tell him there could be no hope of ever improving, but that would be denying him a great deal of personal pleasure and I do not think anyone has the right to do that. So how could one help? There is no one answer, but the first thing to bear in mind is that you hold this person's enjoyment of music for the rest of his life in your hands at this moment. One wrong move and he could be lost, so the answer is to compliment the good things about his playing and slowly begin to explain that there may be some things he could do to improve even more. Hopefully by a process of encouragement, careful explanation and engagement everything will turn out successfully.

Adult 2 was a very musical woman desperately keen to develop her technique to the point that it would be adequate to pass a Licentiate Diploma and gain herself access to a Music Therapy Course. She was already working with music therapy teachers in a number of situations and seemingly doing very well. However, because she did not have a qualification there was no possibility that she would ever get a position teaching herself so she was trying to do the right thing and obtain the qualification.

From the outset I knew that this was going to be a difficult task: she had many obvious bad habits and a few other problems that became apparent as things developed. Tension and incredible nerves, even in lessons, were big problems and the fact that her hands had lost all their suppleness. Progress was very slow, but eventually there was some improvement. The main aid to reducing nerves in this case was continuous and gentle encouragement as well as urging the student to continually reinforce her knowledge of the notes and musical intentions. Knowing the notes securely can reduce nerves dramatically.

Adult 3 comes from a complicated background, upper class yet poor, but has made a considerable success of his life rebuilding the family home and amassing his own fortune. He is a very lively character with many interests and a busy life, but spends a great deal of time with his music and is able to play pieces of some difficulty with varying degrees of success.

He has the same problems that come with age as adult number 2: stiff fingers and considerable nerves. However, there is determination and progress is good much of the time, mainly due to the high level of understanding on his part. The biggest problem is that while progress is evident at home, in lessons (under pressure) his nerves (and consequently breathing) inhibit what he knows could be a good performance. Getting this student to breathe naturally and to take a slightly more comfortable tempo began to reduce his nerves immediately.

You must read what you will into these three cases, but in each one the lesson to be learnt is that you must take every case on its individual merits and think before you act.

Assessment

Assessment, whether one likes or dislikes it, is an integral part of life and in the musical sense it has become an increasingly tricky part of the teaching and learning process. Students are continually assessed and so, quite rightly, are the teachers. This will not faze the good teacher, but it may make the less experienced teacher think a little more constructively.

Much of the assessment we do in our everyday lives is informal and intuitive and often carried out almost subconsciously, but the formal assessment that comes with qualifications is not so easy to deal with. All reputable educational establishments and examining boards provide elaborate criteria for assessment, but it is important that teachers and students have their own criteria and become assessors themselves and of each other. As one becomes more knowledgeable one realises how little one knows, so we must all heighten our awareness and strive to become sensitive and articulate critics and encourage our students to become likewise.

Grade examinations
Grade examinations should not become an end in themselves; they are a challenge, but they will not necessarily make a better player. They can provide a structure for skill and achievement and give a confidence boost as well as some competitive comparison, but unless used wisely, their benefits can be limited. Therefore:
- Consult the syllabus carefully and scrutinise which pieces may or may not be suitable. If a student is ready for the next grade but the pieces are unsuitable do not force the issue simply for the sake of obtaining the grade. Take longer, perhaps skip this grade and go on to the next. This applies to all grades, but particularly grade 6 upwards.
- Some students (especially some teenagers and adults) are more nervous of examinations than others, so try to prepare the pieces without them knowing until they are playing with some confidence and their practice has not been inhibited by the pressure of knowing it is an exam they are working towards. Choices at the higher levels are mostly of pieces available in other forms than the 'exam book'.
- If a student needs an exam grade towards an A level qualification and the pieces of one board are not suitable then try a different board. Some teachers are loathe to do this, preferring to remain loyal to one board, but the needs of the student should come first.

An aide-memoire

How you present your ideas to the more advanced student is perhaps your most important skill and, whilst you will learn many things by trial and error (because we all do), I offer here some suggestions to help you on your way. Some of them you may not agree with and you will almost certainly be able to add to them, but the fact remains that how you come across in your lessons will either produce good results or induce anxiety and unnecessary tension.

- Direct instructions of the 'do this' variety may produce problems. Learn to communicate in a number of different and imaginative ways.
- Avoid contradicting yourself by not giving too many instructions at the same time and never try too hard, it can make the student feel inadequate and is counterproductive.
- Never expect unrealistic standards, this can be damaging.
- Do not be surprised if students forget what you say.
- Be prepared for students to disagree with you, this is good and you can begin a useful discussion.
- Be careful how and when you suggest a student 'tries' something. 'Trying' can suggest lack of ability.
- Help the student to be more aware and notice what they are doing, to pay attention to what is going on and to listen critically.
- Avoid saying something is right or wrong, but do permit students to be wrong – often getting something wrong can produce right.
- Always help students to feel physically comfortable, build rapport and be in sympathy.
- Always check that your students are breathing freely. When anxious or nervous students often forget to breathe without realising.
- Help students to think for themselves by using the Socratic method of question and answer. Always try to develop independence, not dependence and guide them to make their own decisions.
- Be patient.
- Experiment.
- Encourage improvisation since it is a great confidence booster as well as excellent aural training.
- Move ahead at a pace that suits both you and the student.
- Be sensitive to individual issues: some students respond best to direct authoritative guidance whereas others will be happy to take charge.

Further reading

The Inner Game of Music Barry Green with W. Timothy Gallwey (Pan ISBN 0 330300172)

Not Pulling Strings Joseph O'Connor (Kahn & Averill ISBN 0 951215507)

Teaching Music Musically Keith Swanwick (RoutledgeFalmer 0 415199360)

Simon Young
HonFTCL, MPhil, GTCL,
LTCL, LRAM, ARCM,
ARCO
Emeritus Fellow,
Trinity College of Music

supporting skills by Nicholas Keyworth

How to teach the difficult stuff

If, like me, you spend most of the lesson time teaching the instrumental or vocal technique needed to play a piece of music you'll often find there's not enough time for all those other important things: aural skills, music theory, sight reading, improvising, and so on. Where do you start? At least with a piece of music you have the notes in front of you...

The thinking behind this chapter is quite simple – it's an ideas bank. Made up of a number of strategies I have used in my teaching to try and overcome some of the more difficult aspects of instrumental and vocal teaching which are essential to produce a fully rounded musician.

These twelve pages offer you a range of ideas for you and your pupils to try out in lessons. Many of the suggestions are geared towards developing the skills needed for practical music exams. They are designed to work at any level – even the warm-up games should be relevant to pupils of just about any age and ability level.

I hope you will agree that these are useful skills for all students as they grow and develop as musicians. So be experimental! Be bold! And teach the difficult stuff!

> This chapter contains a photocopiable page on each topic for your pupils to use.

Teaching aural

Aural skills are ...
- 'Listening' not merely 'hearing'.
- Analysing what you hear.
- Articulating sounds into words.
- Demonstrating aspects of sounds by singing, clapping or playing.

Encouraging young people to focus intently just on sound can be quite challenging so start by asking them to listen to what is around them. Then they can describe these sounds by:
- Talking about them.
- Drawing them using shapes and squiggles.
- Singing, clapping or playing some of the sounds they heard.

If you teach an instrument that needs tuning up at the start of the lesson, they can be involved in the process from their very first lesson – it's all part of developing listening skills.

Playing with good intonation

There is nothing more likely to kill a lesson dead than to say 'That note is sharp/flat – you're playing out of tune!' or 'Right! Now we're going to do some aural tests.' You need to develop your pupils' 'inner ear' so they can do this themselves. Make up some aural games in your lessons such as:

> **Oops!**
> Play one of your pupil's pieces for them but make some deliberate mistakes. Start simply with a wrong note or rhythm, then progress to changing the articulation or dynamics.
>
> **Secret music**
> Don't let your pupils see a new piece straight away. Instead, play the first few notes and get them to clap the rhythm. Then play it again and ask them to sing it back. Ask them if the notes were loud or soft, *legato, staccato,* and so on. Then tell them the first note and see if they can play the phrase. It's a great way of starting a new piece without getting bogged down with the notation.
>
> **Follow my leader**
> Improvise a simple sound such as a continuous G. Keep repeating it until your pupils join in. Then change to a different sound and repeat it until they catch up... and so on. They are allowed to look at you, but after a while they should only listen!
>
> **Staircase**
> Play up the notes of one of your pupil's scales and stop en route. Ask your pupil to sing the tonic and the note you've reached, then name the interval. Also, start at the top and work downwards.

Aural games

The sound of silence
Stop what you are doing for **one minute**. Write down up to three of the sounds you hear, however quiet:

1. . . . .

2. . . . .

3. . . . .

- On the back of this page draw the sounds by just using simple shapes.
- Try to recreate these sounds on your instrument.
- Organise these ideas into a piece and give it a title.

Compare and contrast
Play the first line of your favourite piece, then ask your teacher to play it to you. Listen carefully and write down three differences that you notice:

1. . . . .

2. . . . .

3. . . . .

When you practise, work on these three things. See if you can change the way you play them ready for your next lesson.

DIY!
Put a clef at the start of the stave below and write a piece to play which:
- Is three bars long.
- Is in $\frac{2}{4}$ time.
- Uses only crotchets (quarter notes) and minims (half notes).
- Starts and ends on the first, third or fifth note of the scale.

Now ask your teacher to give you an aural test based on your piece.

Turn it on!
Choose a CD which you don't listen to very often. Listen to the start of each track twice and then do each of the following:
- Clap the rhythm.
- Sing the melody.
- Identify the opening interval.
- Identify the articulation in the extract.
- Identify the dynamics in the extract.

Teaching sight reading

Is sight reading scary?

We all have an inherent fear of the unknown and it's not unusual for sight reading in an examination to fill even the most confident young musician with trepidation. Why are we so scared of it?

Consider the following questions:
- Are we teaching our pupils to be afraid of making mistakes?
- Do we teach 'the notes' at the expense of fluency?
- Are pupils who regularly play with other musicians better sight-readers?
- Why do we need sight reading in a exam?

Continuity

Most marks are lost for sight reading in exams because pupils think it is more important to play the correct notes than it is to simply play with a sense of continuity! Encourage your pupils to play with a greater musical flow through employing the following strategies:
- *Know your boundaries*: half the battle with sight reading in a examination is knowing what to expect, so look carefully at the parameters in your syllabus. Make sure your pupils understand these along with all the relevant theory.
- *See into the future*: the trick with sight reading is in being able to read the music slightly ahead of where we are playing. We learn this skill when reading text so we can also learn it when reading music. Start with a piece your pupil knows well. Take a small piece of paper or card and move it along the music as they are playing. Start simply by just covering up the note they are playing as soon as they play it so they have to look ahead at the one coming up.
- *Take your partners*: playing some kind of chamber music every lesson illustrates the importance of keeping going rather than hesitating and correcting mistakes. Get some simple duet books to use in your lessons.

Points to remember
- Sight reading tests in exams are usually set at a standard of around two grades lower than the grade being assessed.
- Giving a pupil some practice sight reading in a lesson does not teach them how to do it or how to get better at it!
- Seeing a new piece of music is not the same as looking at it. Train your pupils to search for recognisable shapes and patterns and imagine the sound of music when played.
- In an examination candidates can try out the music during the preparation time. Encourage your pupils to always use this time wisely so it becomes second nature.

Sight reading games

Write your own sight reading

Ask your teacher what the parameters are for the sight reading test in the next grade you are taking. Compose a short piece to play using these parameters on the manuscript paper below. Don't forget to put a clef, a time and a key signature at the beginning. You could also test your friends and your teacher. Give them a mark out of ten!

Did you see?

Look at a new piece (or phrase) of about eight bars and notice the following features. Look away and write down what you remember:

Time signature . . . .

Key signature . . . .

Tempo . . . .

Rhythm patterns . . . .

Pitches . . . .

Accidentals . . . .

Dynamics . . . .

Articulation/phrasing . . . .

The big play through

Dig out some old music you learnt a while ago and play it all through cover to cover. Have a little rest between each piece and write down its title below, but otherwise don't stop: even if you make mistakes!

. . . .

. . . .

. . . .

. . . .

. . . .

. . . .

. . . .

Teaching music theory

Music theory is all about:
- Creating a visual representation of music.
- Relating symbol to sound.
- Understanding and using notation.
- Reading music more effectively.

Linking the eyes and the ears

Encourage pupils to look at music and imagine the sounds represented in the score. Find a new piece of music and ask them questions such as:
- Are there lots of fast or slow notes?
- Where is the melody?
- What do you think it sounds like?

Then play them the piece (or part of it). Ask if it sounded as they expected – if not, in what ways was it different?

Shapes and squiggles
- Find a piece your pupils enjoy playing. Ask them to draw a graphic which shows the first few bars. Then give this graphic to other pupils to play and discuss the differences.
- Draw some graphic shapes and ask your pupils to play them. Then get them to convert what they have played into conventional notation.
- Discuss and explore different ways of interpreting a graphic compared with something written in conventional notation. What are the advantages and disadvantages of each system?

Where am I?

Perform a new piece to your pupil and ask them to follow the music carefully as you play it. Stop suddenly and ask them to point to where you are in the music. This is a way of building a good association between sound and symbol.

Be a composer

Notating a composition is one of the best ways to get people to understand theory. They will make plenty of mistakes initially (particularly with time and rhythm) but they will learn a lot if you correct any notational errors, explaining why as you go. Think of your role as an editor rather than simply looking for mistakes!

It is important that a lesson does not suddenly stop so that the teacher can 'do some theory': that will kill all interest! Theory must be relevant to the instrument being taught and the music being studied. Think how languages are taught successfully using a combination of strategies: sound, written words, pictures – even taste and smell! With a bit of lateral thinking we can adopt similar ideas for our instrumental and vocal tuition.

Music theory games

What's the score?

Look at a piece of music you are studying. In the following chart list as many things as you can find under each title.

Note values	Pitch names	Accidentals
Dynamics	Articulation	Other signs and symbols

Copycat

When you start to learn a new piece, get some manuscript paper and carefully copy out the first phrase. Then check you know and understand all of the following:

- The title of the piece.
- The tempo and tempo description.
- All the pitches and note values.
- The key and time signatures.
- Any repeats.

Compose a piece

Using a piece of manuscript paper, compose an eight bar piece of music using the following elements:

- A clef for your instrument or voice.
- A time signature to show four ♩ beats in each bar.
- A key signature to show the key of D major.
- ♩ ♫ ♩
- The pitches D E F♯ A B in any octave.
- Some *staccato* notes in the middle.
- ***f*** at the start and towards the end.
- A *diminuendo* to ***p*** in the middle followed by a *crescendo*.
- *Rallentando* at the end.

Now play through your piece, then ask your teacher to play it. You could also give a copy to a friend and ask them to play it. Did it always sound the same? If not, note down any differences.

Tell me all

Choose any bar at random from a piece you are currently playing. Talk about everything in that bar (time values, pitch names, articulation, dynamics, tempo, key and so on). More advanced pupils can choose a phrase rather than bar.

Teaching improvisation

Effective improvisers:

- Can respond with spontaneity.
- Are comfortable with their instruments/voice.
- Can play with a musical sense of style.
- Can create music with a sense of musical shape.

Why bother?

Much of our teaching time is spent ensuring our pupils play the right notes, but this can often be a barrier to playing with fluency and musical conviction. That's why I believe improvisation is so important, as it can encourage a real sense of musical continuity and creativity together with a natural empathy with an instrument.

Asking a young musician to 'just play anything' will usually just get a blank look in response. We need to give some musical starting points for them to respond to such as:

- A graphic.
- A musical question.
- A notated stimulus.

Rather than just playing a scale as a warm-up exercise at the start of a lesson, try some improvisation games to encourage them to play more freely, open their ears and switch on their minds. Here are some ideas for improvisation games you can use in your lessons:

What's the answer?

Play some simple musical 'questions' to your pupils (perhaps one or two bars). Do not be tempted to work these out and write them down beforehand: you must improvise as well! Ask your pupils to respond by playing an 'answer' to your question. Start with simple crotchets and gradually increase the difficulty in rhythm and length. Try to encourage your pupils to bring the music to a natural close at the end and make sure the overall result is musically balanced.

Flash cards

Create a series of flash cards – each one containing a simple single image such as a wavy line, a star or a big black blob. Ask your pupils to play a sound which represents the image on the card. Analyse the response with your pupils by discussing musical elements such as choice of pitch, duration and dynamics, then play it again. You could ask pupils to arrange the cards in a sequence to make a piece of music and give it a title.

Starting points

Give your pupil any three pitches, or a simple three note rhythm, or three chords, or a simple sentence (for singers). Explore how this could become the opening of a piece of music. Try to do this by playing or singing rather than by talking about it.

Improvisation games

Musical ideas

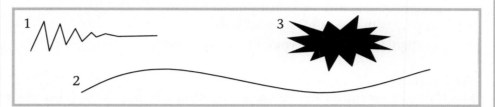

Here are three graphics. For each one think about:
- How loud or soft it is.
- How fast or slow it is.
- How high or low it is.

Try playing or singing each one. Next turn the shapes into a short piece of music by repeating some of them, changing the order and perhaps varying the way you interpret them. Write down the order below, repeating ideas as many times as you like.

. . . .

. . . .

Ideas bank

Play through each of these musical ideas with your instrument. Choose one you like and develop it to create a short piece of music. Don't forget to give it an ending!

Pitch *Hint*: give your piece a lively rhythm	*Rhythm* *Hint*: give your piece a melody (unless you're a percussionist!)
Chords *Hint*: give your piece a lively rhythm or add a melody on top	*Words* Sunday is the laziest day of the week *Hint*: remember to include melody and rhythm

New directions

Take a piece you can play but after the first one or two bars let the piece take a different path.

See if you can bring the new piece to a logical conclusion.

Teaching composition

In a sense, the next stage on from improvising is composing. The major differences are:

- Improvising can be instant, composing can be thought through.
- Composing can be notated.
- A composition can be replicated by someone else.

Composing can be a very useful activity to encourage:

- An understanding of the capabilities of the instrument or voice.
- An understanding of notation.
- The development and reworking of musical ideas.
- An understanding of structure, shape and style.

Build some strategies into your lessons to encourage composing, such as:

Composing together

Using simple notes and rhythms:

- You compose a first bar, play it, write it down and hand it to your pupil.
- They play it back and compose the second bar. They play it, write it down and hand it to you.
- You play it and compose the third bar... and so on until you come to a natural close.
- You could do this in groups as well, going round the circle taking it in turns.

Analysis

Making a recording of a pupil's improvisation can be a very useful starting point to composing. By listening to it together, pupils can analyse the actual piece (not the playing of it) by answering the following questions:

- Did you enjoy listening to the piece?
- What style is it in?
- How is it structured?
- How would you make it longer?

Ternary form

Find a phrase that your pupils can already play or sing well. Call this *section A*. Ask them to compose a contrasting *section B* before repeating *section A* again. Get them to write it down in some form. Record your pupil playing the result.

It is daunting to simply be given a blank sheet of manuscript paper and told to go and compose something. Give your pupils some parameters to work within. Discuss a brief with them, including information such as:

Title • Mood • Instrumentation • Length • Structure • Difficulty

---

Composition games

Building blocks

Here are some musical ideas you can use to make a composition. First, work out what you can do for each musical idea using your instrument or voice, then put them together in any order you like. Write down your order below, repeating the ideas as many times as you like.

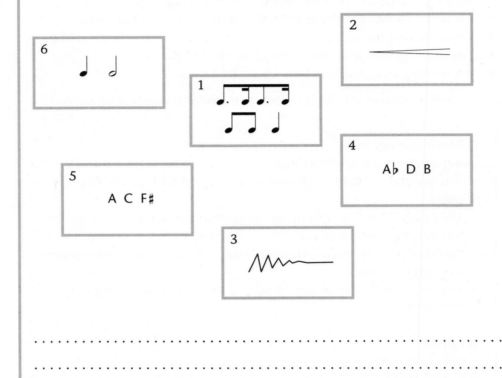

. . . .

. . . .

On the line

Compose a single line melody for your instrument or voice based on the graphics below. You can think of the graphics as representing either the pitch, the dynamics or the speed.

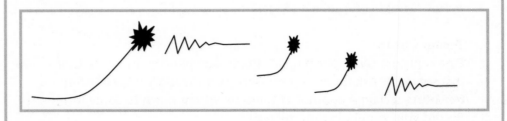

Write it down

Think of a piece you know from memory: try to write it down without looking at the music. If there are any parts you cannot remember, compose some new music to fill the gaps!

Some examination boards such as Trinity Guildhall allow candidates to perform one of their own compositions as one of their examination pieces.

Teaching vocal skills

It's all very well incorporating some of the new techniques included in this chapter into your lessons but I'm sure you have some pupils who just will not sing. There may be many reasons for this such as:

- General shyness.
- Lack of vocal ability.
- Changing voices.

For candidates taking aural tests in an examination situation this can cause real anxiety. But even pupils who don't take exams are missing out on a real opportunity to internalise music in a way they can't do through their instrument.

This is not about singing lessons – it is to do with empowering pupils to have the confidence to use their voices as a useful tool in understanding the music they are playing more fully.

It's not much good just saying 'Come on, sing it!' to a shy teenager, but there are several strategies you can use to start to encourage your pupils to use their voices with assurance. Try out some of these ideas for starters:

> **Scat!**
> Choose a rhythmic piece your pupil can play well and pick one phrase. Speak the rhythms using scat words such as:
>> *Doo be dah, she ba*
>> *Shoobedy wop, doo dah*
>
> This can be great fun if you add a backing rhythm to it from a keyboard. You could also get pupils in a group to take a phrase in turn. This will help all of them to internalise the music they are working on.
>
> **Within range**
> Get your pupils to sing the first phrase of a piece they are working on, but start on any note they feel comfortable with, even if it is very low. This may mean they hum a note to start with and you find it on your instrument or piano. This should keep it within your pupil's vocal range. Remember when humming to keep the mouth slightly open, saying *nn* rather than *mm,* as this is slightly easier.
>
> **Call and response**
> We used call and response as a strategy to help with improvisation in *What's the answer?* Try throwing in the occasional vocal question as well – perhaps by initially using scat or humming – they may answer using their instrument, but you never know...

Make sure you give plenty of support and always encourage them at the end to build their confidence, otherwise any activity will seem like a test!

Vocal games

By ear

Who is your favourite singer? Write their name down here:

. . . .

And what is the title of your favourite song? Write the name down here:

. . . .

Try singing the beginning to yourself. Think about the shape of the vocal line and then see if you can play it on your instrument. It may take a while to get the notes exactly correct but with patience you will do it. Just concentrate on the opening phrase if you like.

La dee da

Choose a piece you enjoy playing with a good melody (percussionists think of some good rhythmic patterns you enjoy playing). Work out some lyrics to fit the melody. Try singing them out loud. Perform the song to your friends or teacher if you dare!

Lyrics:. . . . .

. . . .

. . . .

. . . .

. . . .

Phrase by phrase

Find a simple piece, like a folk tune, that you know really fluently.

- Divide it up into phrases or musical sentences.

- Play the first phrase then sing it back straight away. Do the same with the next phrase and so on.

- Now do it the other way around, sing the first phrase then play it back straight away; do the same with the next phrase, and so on.

Nicholas Keyworth
BAHons (Bath), DipHE
Senior examiner,
Trinity Guildhall

Further reading

Getting started with aural Nicholas Keyworth (Trinity Faber ISBN 0571521371)

Getting started with composition Paul Harris
(Trinity Faber ISBN 057152236X)

Getting started with keyboard musicianship Nicholas Keyworth
(Trinity Faber ISBN 0571521363)

Getting started with theory Nicholas Keyworth (Trinity Faber ISBN 0571521959)

Examination preparation and nerves *by Nicholas Keyworth*

Let's consider why we enter our pupils for examinations in the first place. They can create important goals when learning an instrument, allowing candidates to perform something that they have prepared over a period of time to the best of their ability and with confidence and a sense of enjoyment. Some pupils love the opportunity to perform but others are less sure. This chapter looks at different strategies which may help the latter.

It is important to point out that an examination is not a competition or a race. We are not saying that the first person to perform correctly wins a prize. However they play, pupils can be sure of a welcome, a focused and discerning ear, and a thoughtful, positive and constructive response. Examiners do actually enjoy hearing people play! We want to hear people giving us their best and we will do all we can to help people feel comfortable and welcome.

An examination is, in some way, a snapshot, a quick overview of a candidate's musical achievement done in a short space of time in a strange room in front of another musician. Some candidates may have been working towards this examination for just a few weeks, other for a few years. Some are very young and others are more mature. For some the sense of performance comes naturally but for others it is a real effort. In every case the approach from the examiner is the same – to give a genuine welcome and a warm invitation to perform to the best of their ability, and to receive a fair, balanced assessment of the performance.

How you can help

Know the syllabus

Any experienced teacher realises how important it is to know a syllabus inside out before embarking on a programme of study leading to an exam. A syllabus is much more than a list of pieces. It gives information on:

- Different options we can select according to our pupils' abilities and interests, such as the opportunity for candidates to perform their own compositions.
- The parameters for the supporting tests.
- Criteria by which the performance will be assessed – invaluable for judging when your pupils are ready for the next grade.

To make sure the structure of the examination is known and understood, try some of these ideas in your lessons:

- Run a mock examination with your pupils. Mark them according to the criteria and share the results with them at the end.
- Use the parameters for the supporting tests as simple composition exercises so your pupils can write their own sample tests.
- Share the marking criteria with your pupils so they can understand what they need to do to improve their performance – rather than relying on you to tell them every time!

What pieces am I playing?

It is amazing how many pupils prepare for an examination without even knowing the titles of their pieces. At higher grades many candidates don't know the composer or basic background information about their pieces, such as when and why the music was written. This important knowledge places the piece in context and encourages an understanding of style and musical conventions. How many of the following questions can your pupils answer about their pieces – *without looking at the music?*

Know your piece

The title . . . .

The name of the composer . . . .

A word to describe the mood . . . .

The tempo and first note at the start . . . .

The key and time signatures . . . .

The period of the music and approximate date of composition . . . .

What do they have to do to pass?

Candidates do not have to pass every section in an examination to pass the whole thing. It is the total mark that counts and many candidates 'fluff' one or two areas (sight reading and aural can often be the weakest) but succeed overall because the other sections of the examination are stronger. Of the relatively small number of pupils who do not reach the required standard in an examination the majority try again and pass well on a second attempt. The most common reasons for not passing include:

- **Unrhythmic playing:** make sure there is a sense of pulse in every performance; play with crisp rhythms.
- **Hesitant playing:** aim for fluency. Technical security and knowing all the notes in the piece are essential.
- **Poor tone and intonation:** make sure the playing is in tune and has a well-focused sound.
- **Lack of performance:** a sense of communication is essential for a good performance so ensure the playing projects to its audience.

Using the criteria

Look at the criteria in the syllabus with your pupils. Make sure they understand what is required to pass, to get a merit and to get a distinction. Now ask them to play one of their pieces and then try to get them to match some of the phrases in the criteria to their playing. It is unlikely that you will find their performance fits neatly into one of the bands so you will have to find a 'best match'. Make a short list of what needs to be done to raise the performance up to the next level. If you teach in a group then get the other pupils to give their opinions too!

Don't forget the supporting tests

As teachers we naturally tend to focus more on the pieces than on the other components in the examination. I know there is only limited time in a music lesson to get through everything. Sometimes we can only find time to 'test' sight-reading and aural rather than actually teach them. This leads to candidates being unprepared in one or more areas, and the attitude that that 'you can either do it or you can't'. This generates anxiety about the whole examination, which can have a detrimental effect on the areas they can do well! They must be well prepared for every part of an examination.

I find the easiest and quickest way to prepare candidates for the supporting tests is through the warm-up at the start of a lesson – or at the end as means of consolidating what has been learnt. Here are some examples:

---

supporting tests ideas

Technical work
  Play the scales in the keys of the pieces they are learning, using some fun rhythms.
Sight reading
  Play a simple duet with your pupil as a warm-up piece, and don't let them stop!
Aural skills
  As they walk through the door, play the first few bars of one of their pieces and get them to clap it, sing it, and describe various aspects of it.
Viva voce
  Ask them what they can remember about their pieces before they get their music out!
Improvisation
  Play some call and response games, or improvise a complete piece.

Examination nerves

Nervous pupils are often more afraid of the unknown in an examination rather than the actual assessment itself. Here are some ideas to turn it into a more positive experience and ensure nerves do not spoil an otherwise successful performance.

- Make sure your pupils have plenty of opportunities to perform for other people. An examination is essentially another performance.
- Candidates should always warm-up before they go into the examination room. Don't worry about being overheard.
- Encourage your pupils to say something to the examiner when they walk in. A warm smile and a 'good morning' is a good start.
- Pupils should focus on performing music rather than on thinking about themselves or the examiner.
- Candidates can take the different components of the examination in any order, so they can start with their technical work, for example.
- Make sure your pupils do not expect to get everything right. Some fall to pieces as soon as they make their first mistake – so use the criteria to help them realise that it's not all about perfection.
- Remember that nerves can be a good thing. If all that energy and adrenaline is channelled in a positive way it can actually enhance a performance.

Always remember to put examinations in perspective, and don't forget that an examination syllabus is not a teaching syllabus.

Nicholas Keyworth
BAHons (Bath), DipHE
Senior examiner,
Trinity Guildhall

© 2005 by Nicholas Keyworth

Motivational teaching and optimal learning

by Sara Shaw and Trevor Hawes

Beliefs and values

Individual beliefs and values are an important aspect of learning which is not always accorded the significance it deserves.

The human brain is a multi-processor, analysing huge quantities of incoming data every minute, and working on various levels simultaneously. Some scientists suggest that the brain may in some respects be organised in a hierarchical way.

Robert Dilts' concept of neurological levels* offers a model which can be used to shed light on some of the dynamics which influence learning.
The neurological levels include:

- Self identity (Who am I?)
- Beliefs/values (Why do I do what I do?)
- Capabilities (How do I do what I do?)
- Performance/behaviour (What do I do?)
- Environment (Where and when do I do it?)

...**The Reptilian Brain** plays an important role in brain function and is very concerned with **environmental** issues. Teachers in many schools face considerable environmental challenges, with poor working conditions and limited resources. In order to learn, certain types of **behaviour** are required – not just reflex actions in response to teacher-led tasks (such as filling in a worksheet) but putting learning to some active use.

Capabilities are the link between beliefs and values and behaviour. Capabilities allow us to translate our beliefs and values into behaviour. The capability to learn is shared by all the human race.

Our **beliefs and values** determine why we learn – in other words what motivates us. This level is of fundamental importance in its influence on learning. Different cultural or gender values may lead to different approaches or emphases in learning (e.g. men don't read, it's not important to come to school on time).

Our beliefs and values stem from our sense of **identity** – who we perceive ourselves to be. Sometimes someone's sense of identity inhibits them from learning because they think that if they acquire a particular capability it will make them someone they don't want to be (e.g. a swot, a 'boff'). Sometimes we unintentionally create an identity for a child (dyslexic, a problem child).

An understanding of the dynamics between the different neurological levels can be helpful in deciding what would be the most effective way of tackling a problem. If a child has trouble learning to spell, it is because they are using an ineffective strategy or because they have an unuseful (limiting) belief – e.g. spelling is really difficult, no-one in our family can spell. Or maybe they have taken on an identity – I am a bad speller.

Traditionally, teaching has tended to be focused on the capability and behaviour levels and may have not paid sufficient attention to the powerful influence belief and identity issues can have on a child's achievements.

Children need to establish strong positive identities as learners so that they feel free to take risks and fully participate in [classroom] activities rather than falling back on self-protection strategies. Teachers can help by tackling limiting beliefs (including their own), maintaining the highest expectations, and working to build self-esteem.

10 tips for memorable teaching

A brain is able to retain and recall information that:

1 *Is presented in short bursts.* We remember far more of the information from the start and finish of presentations and tend to forget the bits in between. Try to break up a teaching session into mini sessions, thereby maximising the number of starts and finishes.

2 *Is regularly reviewed.* Research shows that up to 80% of information may be forgotten if it is not reviewed. Teachers should plan to review key facts at least five times during the lesson and briefly the following day, week and month. Use questions and quizzes to review material.

3 *Engages the emotions.* The strength of the neural connections made when the emotions are aroused is significantly greater. It is as if the brain puts down a marker to say this experience (e.g. touching a hot kettle for the first time) is worth remembering. The emotional content of lessons can be increased through the use of humour, creating anticipation.

4 *Is used to construct meaning.* Making information mean something to oneself increases both the strength and number of neural connections – thereby aiding recall. For example, a child is far more likely to remember what they have learnt about electricity of they are given the opportunity to make and break a circuit. A very effective way to facilitate the construction of meaning is to get a child to explain to someone else what they have learnt.

5 *Is multi-sensory thereby utilising several memory systems.* It has been suggested that we remember 20% of what we read, 30% of what we hear, 40% of what we see, 50% of what we say, 60% of what we do and 90% of what we read, hear, see, say and do!

6 *Is presented in context.* When information is presented in a supporting context the brain makes more associations and constructs more meaning. This makes data more memorable. Children will recall field trips when other lessons have been long forgotten.

7 *Engages both hemispheres.* That we find it easier to remember the lyrics to songs than the words to poems is due to the fact singing stimulates both hemispheres (words/left brain and music/right brain). Whole brain activities include drawing concept maps, using rhyme and rhythm when reciting facts (e.g. times tables) or playing baroque music in the background when reviewing data.

8 *Is relevant or important to the individual.* The brain is selective about the information it transfers to long term memory. Items of data that are important or relevant to a child are far more likely to be remembered. Identify and explain why it is important to remember the key facts and make them relevant to the child.

9 *Connects to prior knowledge.* The more associations or connections we can make between a new item of data and things we already know, the easier it is ro recall. E.g. Clouds are made up of water vapour – like steam from a kettle. [Topic work is particularly useful in enabling associations or connections to be made.]

10 *Employs memory strategies.* We remember the five features of good targets through associating it with the word SMART (Specific, Measurable, Achievable, Reviewed and Timetabled). If you needed to remember the PIN number for your cash card was 5487, using the phrase 'Money From Electric Machine' (which has 5 letters, 4 letters, 8 letters, 7 letters) makes the numbers much more memorable. Use memory strategies or mnemonics to ensure information is retained and recalled.

Optimal learning – putting it all together

1 Establish an appropriate learning environment
Take all possible steps to ensure children's physical and emotional well-being. Pupils need to feel safe and secure and have a sense of belonging. They need to have high self-esteem and a strong belief in themselves as learners. They need to have a positive feeling about the learning opportunities they are about to face, know that they will be challenged and that they will succeed.

2 Connect the learning
Learning is most effective when the student is able to connect what is being learned today with knowledge and understanding that has previously been developed. Brain compatible teaching includes starting lessons by reviewing ground that has been previously covered and explaining how new material builds on this.

3 Paint the big picture
Learners, particularly those who favour their right hemisphere, will benefit from the whole lesson being outlined at the beginning – a bit like being shown the lid of a jigsaw before starting to assemble the puzzle.

4 Define the learning objectives
It is important that the teacher has clearly defined learning objectives for the session and shares these with the pupils. Ensure that pupils are motivated to learn by explaining *what's in it for me* and *connecting into their values.*

5 Present information
Research shows that we each have our personal style of learning. Present information in a way that reaches a variety of learning styles so that there is something for everyone. Providing information which is relevant, interesting and has an emotional contents will ensure it is more memorable. Remember that the neo-cortex works best in short bursts of concentration.

6 Increase knowledge and understanding
To turn knowledge into understanding, pupils need to construct their own

meaning from the information they receive. An appropriate activity will allow this opportunity – especially if it encourages pupils to process information through one of the seven intelligences.

7 Demonstrating knowledge and understanding

Ultimately students will be required to show what they know. Explaining a concept to a peer or adult is one powerful way of consolidating learning. Providing opportunities for assessment through different intelligences raises self-esteem for children with strengths in areas other than the linguistic or logical mathematical.

8 Reviewing for recall and retention

Review is a vital part of ensuring that knowledge and understanding are transferred to long term memory. A regular review cycle will increase recall and retention.

9 Feedback

Regular and immediate feedback dramatically improves learning. Build in feedback mechanisms which include self and peer evaluation. Encourage students to recognise and celebrate reaching goals and targets and to share effective learning strategies with each other.

10 Preview

The speed at which new concepts are learnt can be increased if they are previewed in advance. Teachers could usefully spend the first lesson of each year previewing the whole year's curriculum and the last few minutes of each lesson previewing the next.

Three short extracts taken from
Effective Teaching and Learning in the Primary Classroom by Sara Shaw and Trevor Hawes (Optimal Learning ISBN 0-9533531-0-9)

* see *Dynamic Learning* Dilts & Epstein 1995

Sara Shaw and Trevor Hawes
Senior consultants, Optimal Learning Group

Top practice tips *by Mark Stringer*

Motivating your pupils to practise is one of the trickiest aspects of instrumental teaching. Here are a range of strategies to pass on to your pupils, to be varied according to their ability, age and personality and also to keep their interest going when they encounter problems. **Don't let them believe that practising is boring: it should be fun and fulfilling!**

- Think of your brain as a **computer**: what you load into it is what you will reproduce.

- Practice is **preparation**, it's the only way to develop your skills and work towards a performance, just as training is preparation for an athlete.

> Plan your practice carefully – this is quality time and it is important that you make the most of it. Think of long, medium and short term goals. They must be achievable – don't be too ambitious!

- Be clear about **what you want to achieve** in each practice session.

- Try to establish a **practice routine**: practising every evening after work or school, or in the morning before you leave home. Everyone is different so find out what works best for you.

- **Short, focused and frequent practice sessions** of say 15 minutes are usually more effective than irregular, lengthy practice slots BUT do practise every day if at all possible.

- A practice session should be stimulating so make sure you work on a **variety of skills**: include technical work as well as working on pieces.

- **Always break down passages you are working on into bite-sized chunks.** You can break down complex sections into more simple strands: for example, on the piano work on left hand/right hand lines in the score separately before putting them together.

- Ideally, a practice session should involve working on pieces at **different stages of preparation**: a new piece, a piece you have been working on for a while (for which you know the notes and are working on musical aspects) and a piece in which you are polishing the detail.

- When practising **be patient** and learn notes very slowly, double-checking to make sure they are correct. Learning music correctly will save you so much time. It takes at least 20 repetitions to correct a mistake learnt previously.

- **Avoid wasting time.** It's all too easy to start playing through pieces instead of working on the areas you need to focus on. Identify the difficulties you need to work on in a piece of music and stick to these.

- **If you make a mistake** when you are practising, stop and practise this section at a slower tempo. Play it over and over again correctly to eradicate the mistake from your memory.

If there is a passage which you are really struggling with, compose your own exercise which uses the same techniques you need to master, and work on this exercise away from the piece until you have overcome the challenges, then return to the music itself.
Take the tricky phrase and try varying:
- the rhythm
- the articulation
- the dynamics
- the tempo

There are many more possibilities: you can develop exercises to tackle any challenges you face in a piece of music whether they are rhythmical, technical or artistic.

- **Experiment with different ways to learn pieces.** You could try learning a piece from the end and work back rather than from the beginning.

- **Remember that progress is not a steady learning curve.** There will be times when you feel that you are not making headway, but this will pass if you carry on working!

- Don't forget that what you achieve in one piece of music will be a **transferable skill** to other music.

- Remember that few things in life which are worth achieving can be attained overnight!

Practising technical work
- Make sure your exercises are focused directly on the skills you need to develop.
- Always start to practise slowly and gradually build up speed. Use a metronome to increase the tempo gradually. You should start at a slower speed than the tempo you built up to in your last practice session.
- Maintain a relaxed posture at all times – tension can cause injury. If you every start to feel pain, stop!

Don't just practise something until you can play it: practise it until it can't go wrong!

Further reading
The Practice Revolution: Getting great results from the six days between music lessons
 Philip Johnson (Practicespot Press ISBN 095819050X) www.practicespot.com

How to get your Child to Practise... Cynthia Richards (Advance Arts & Music
 ISBN 097293961X)

Mark Stringer
GMusRNCM(Hons) FTCL
ARCM ARCO(CHM)
PGCE FRSA
Director of Performing
Arts Examinations,
Trinity Guildhall

Ensembles and concerts

by Nigel Stubbs

One of the most satisfying aspects of a teacher's life is to see individuals meeting and performing music together. This is surely what instrumental playing is all about, the ability to share and appreciate the joy and fun one gets from performing together.

Getting started with ensembles

From personal experience I have found that children benefit greatly from playing in an ensemble in the early stages. It is not beyond the realms of possibility for children to participate in some form of ensemble after only a few months of tuition, providing the part is appropriate for them and the director of the group is of a sympathetic nature. In fact, for very young children, written music would be of a very basic nature or not even required at all, with the emphasis very much on memory work and varied musical activities. They will be learning:

• Tuning and listening.
• Watching and communication.
• The social side (and when not to talk!).
• Presentation and performing to others.

If you form an ensemble in a small primary school, the chances are your instrumentalists will be of a diverse nature. There could be recorder players, four violinists, one cellist, eight clarinetists and a beginner trumpeter! Although this is not a standard ensemble format there are publications that cater for different instruments at different levels of ability. These 'flexible arrangements' have melody in C parts that could be played by recorders, flutes and violins, and parts specifically for transposing instruments. There are also parts for bass clef instruments and a piano part to fill in the gaps or cover up any exposed parts! However, you will often have to write or adapt a part in order to include certain individuals (see section on arranging below).

Tips for getting started
• Establish a regular day and time for practices and try to stick to this.
• Make sure a suitable room is available for your rehearsals. Nothing is more frustrating than having to move everyone out because someone else has booked the room!
• Make sure you have more than enough parts for the children you expect to attend. Having three or four violinists sitting at one music stand is definitely not good practice.
• Remember that photocopying is subject to restrictions. Check this carefully.

Be prepared to start in a humble fashion. The actual gathering of players in the early stages is more important than the musical result. Over time you will discover which pupils will cope with more adventurous parts, thus creating a more substantial and interesting timbre and texture.

Directing ensembles

We have already touched on some approaches when starting a brand new ensemble particularly with younger players. However, there are standard procedures that we should all try to bear in mind when taking a rehearsal. 'Getting it right' will go a long way towards making good musical progress and creating a happy and purposeful atmosphere. I've found the following to be useful when taking rehearsals:

- Get there early so that you are ready to start on time. Some pupils love to help in the setting up process – encourage this. You will also have time to welcome any new members who may be feeling a little nervous.
- Sketch a rough seating plan in order to avoid confusion when players arrive. This can be open to review but at least you can get everyone sat down and started.
- Be organised and be prepared: decide what you wish to achieve by the end of each rehearsal.
- Be patient: do not forget your own humble beginnings, when you were put at the back of the section and managed only a few notes in an entire rehearsal!
- Be enthusiastic but purposeful. If you are not enjoying yourself then don't expect the ensemble to.
- Finally, do not overlook the social aspects of music making. Breaks are important for all! Pupils who are given time to make new friends through music are much more likely to attend rehearsals regularly.

Conducting and rehearsing: the practicalities

Most conductors have an instrumental specialism that they are particularly knowledgeable about and most comfortable with. However, it really is incumbent on any conductor to have at least a 'working knowledge' of the other instruments in the ensemble.

An example of this is in assisting pupils in tuning their instruments. At its most basic level this could be telling a clarinetist to 'pull out' (making the instrument longer, when they are sharp). Tuning string instruments can cause major headaches for a non-string specialist. Don't forget that adjusters (where fitted) solve the problem when the instrument is only slightly out of tune but more care is required when using the pegs. A quick word with colleagues will fill you in with the essentials. After a few goes you will be tuning even the most temperamental cello like a seasoned pro!

We are much less likely to run away from tackling difficult areas if we have at least a basic understanding of what to expect from young instrumentalists and some simple technical advice to offer them.

Rehearsal tips

- Insist on good posture when rehearsing. You don't suddenly acquire it at the concert! This also supports the work of instrumental teachers who constantly have to reinforce this very important area. Good posture not only looks impressive but more importantly helps to project a better sound.

- Establish a procedure for tuning. If a piano is being used then you will have to use this as the basis for tuning up. Insisting on quiet will encourage everyone to listen carefully, which will benefit aural awareness. I prefer to tune by families from the highest down to the lowest instrument.

- Make brief notes on what you have rehearsed just as you would after giving an instrumental lesson. If certain passages cause a real problem, make a note of these and ask a specialist for any fingering or technical help you could pass on to pupils at the next rehearsal.

- Create a style: your preparatory beat and body language should reflect not only the correct tempo but also the style and mood of the piece. An upbeat with the dynamism of a wet lettuce will not encourage your ensemble to start their march *ff* as indicated.

- Split difficult passages into small manageable chunks.

- Slow practice: remember the old saying 'don't run before you can walk'. So often this is overlooked with an orchestra playing at top speed right from the first rehearsal. This results in mistakes being firmly embedded in the brain from the very first note! It will prove almost impossible to remove these in subsequent rehearsals.

- Practise unison passages for accuracy of intonation, balance, phrasing and articulation.

- Identify inconsistencies such as variations in articulation. Are the wind and brass both supposed to tongue or slur? Are the strings bowing correctly?

- Whole sections with a syncopated part often cause problems. Find another part that is playing on the beat and practise these two together. This may seem rather obvious with the score in front of you but pupils can get so bogged down with their own part that they miss where the help can come from.

- Playing through an entire piece and then starting again from the beginning is unlikely to inspire anyone. On the other hand if you rarely get to figure 1 each week everyone will be in for a white knuckle ride on the day of the concert!

- Be sure that when sections are being rehearsed the other players listen attentively and are aware of how their part fits into the whole picture. Learning to listen is good general discipline for all musicians.

- Occasionally try changing the seating around to give the players a different perspective. Share opportunities: flute 2 could play flute 1 in a piece and so on. This will give invaluable experience and goes some way to dissolving the 'pecking order' feuds that can simmer away in some ensembles.

- There is usually a way to make a balanced ensemble. If there is a shortage of viola players, for example, make some instruments available so that 3 or 4 violinists can play viola for one piece. If you have the instruments you could do this with different players for each piece.

Dynamics
Establish the range of dynamics in a piece and assign a number to each one:

Level 6:   *ff*
Level 5:   *f*
Level 4:   *mf*
Level 3:   *mp*
Level 2:   *p*
Level 1:   *pp*

Now ask the ensemble to do the following:
1. Play as loudly as possible – call this level 6.
2. Play as softly as possible – call this level 1.
3. Work out what levels 2, 3 and 4 would be.

Move freely between each dynamic level to reinforce the sound levels. I have found this helps to internalise the different levels in a fun and practical way and it works! This needs to be practised on a regular basis so that adjusting to different dynamic levels becomes second nature.

Rehearsal activities

Sometimes it can be useful to try some different activities if only to keep everybody on their toes. A different approach can be all that is needed to solve a specific problem. Try the following at your next rehearsal:

- **Clap rhythms** when difficulty arises. This can be great fun, especially if you incorporate the dynamics, and stand up to indicate a rest. Try clapping using different timbres as well: with hands on knees or tapping on the cheeks, for example. Develop this further by having one section clapping a steady pulse whilst the others clap the written rhythm.

- **Sing the parts** wherever possible – this goes a long way to internalising the pitch and improving intonation. Don't under estimate the use of the voice. It is a very powerful and expressive tool and creates a firm foundation for improving musicality.

- **Make the players with the melody stand up** when they are in the spotlight so that the musical structure is visual as well as aural.

- **Get willing players to come out and conduct** and insist that the players follow the beat. This works even better if you are then able to participate as an instrumentalist.

- **Scrambling the players** can be very interesting: move everyone around so that they do not sit next to anyone else in their section. This really tests the ability of a player to 'hold' their part.

Score reading

A little preparation prior to conducting a new piece can go a long way in helping you get the best results. With more complex arrangements it is important to know where the most significant thematic material occurs so that you can direct in a fluent and confident manner. Similarly, when an instrument has been resting for numerous bars it is helpful if you are able to 'wake them up' a couple of bars or so before their next entry. Here are a few practical ideas:

- Mark the main entries on your score so that you can see them coming.
- Make sure you write down whatever directions you give during a rehearsal so that future rehearsals are consistent. On too many occasions I have been told by the conductor that a 'bar for nothing' will be given only to find this doesn't happen in the concert!
- If your group contains transposing instruments make sure you know

what pitch to expect to hear when you ask for a specific passage to be played.

Arranging for ensembles

Arranging music can be extremely useful, satisfying and often essential. At times we need to write or adapt parts appropriate to a child's need in order to achieve a musically satisfying outcome. The availability of music software has made the process of arranging so much easier and quicker. A simple third flute part can become an even simpler fourth flute part by a few clicks of the mouse, and you can save them both!

> At this stage a word of caution needs to be added about adapting or arranging parts. If you have purchased a set of parts, then adapting some of them to suit the abilities of your own pupils will not usually present a problem with the publisher. However, it is always wise to contact the publisher to see if there are any copyright issues you have overlooked, particularly if there are plans to record the performance.
>
> If you wish to make any form of arrangement of a work protected by copyright, permission must be obtained from the publisher. Copyright in music usually lasts for 70 years after a composer's death, so this includes pop, jazz, musicals, recent classical music, film music and so on. Arrangements are copyright, too, so this also applies if you are making an arrangement of an arrangement! If in doubt, check with the publishers copyright department.

The basics

Make sure you have at least a working knowledge of the instruments you are arranging for and the standard of the players. A trumpeter playing for a year could possibly manage a range of a sixth from a written G above middle C descending, for example. On the other hand, beginner violinists are happiest playing in D major and most will be able to manage the notes of this scale in the register just above middle C.

A lot will depend on how pupils are taught and this influences what you are able to write for them. With young brass players in particular the method of tuition may mean that you have to write in the treble or bass clef and this has a bearing on the transposition required. This area can be a minefield and it is always best to consult the instrumental teacher. I have often listened to instrumental teachers who have showed concern (and this is putting it mildly) over the parts their pupils have to play and how inappropriate they are. We can all be guilty of not sharing information and liaison between all music teachers is an essential ingredient to solving the problems that occur.

> ### Tips for arranging
> - Include rests in parts: players need them and it also makes them count!
> - Do try to share the melody around. Everyone likes his or her moment of glory! So often only the best players get the tune. It does not give much encouragement to a young inexperienced

player if their part is an accompaniment all the time. Also it often takes a more experienced player to play the accompaniment parts.

- Mix things around: give the first violin part to the second and the violas or cellos, or the clarinet part to the saxophone.
- Remember to work out transpositions carefully where appropriate. Handing out exactly the same part to first violins and first clarinet in B flat will result in some particularly nasty sounds! If a string part is in C major then the clarinet and trumpet parts will have to be in D major to work together.

Problems to bear in mind

- With mixed ensembles (such as junior orchestras), **keys** can be a problem. Flat keys are more appropriate for beginner wind players, so you may have to be selective with the notes you choose to give other instruments. Violin and viola players will not come across flats for quite a while, but it is still possible to play in flat keys providing you are selective about the harmony notes you give them. However, double bass players often start in ½ position, in which case they are more familiar with B flat major.
- **String crossing** also needs to be managed properly; passages which alternate notes on different strings can be straightforward if the strings are adjacent (e.g. D to A). Encourage players to practise such passages slowly, only use small amounts of bow and to keep the wrist flexible.
- **Repeated notes** can be difficult for wind players before they've mastered their tonguing technique, so don't overdo *staccato* passages!
- Remember that brass players like to play fast and loud! **High notes** are difficult for them to play quietly and anything much more than an octave above middle C for a trumpet will quickly swamp all the other players.
- Be aware of technical problems related to specific instruments, for example the **break on a clarinet**. Find out if they have played above the break and whether they can play notes around the break with relative ease.
- It is worthwhile finding out whether your string players have done any work in **higher positions**. If they haven't, the highest note a violinist can play is the B immediately above the treble clef, and for viola players E immediately above the alto clef. More advanced players will have a knowledge beyond 3rd position (violin) and 4th position (cello).

Putting together a successful concert

Planning ahead

There seem to be so many different things to organise that putting on any concert can cause a major headache, particularly if a lot of students are involved. However, with careful planning many potential problems can be resolved easily.

A large-scale event obviously has the potential to cause problems, but even a small informal occasion needs to be planned carefully in order for it to run smoothly. I have been involved in organising all kinds of events from a handful of pupils playing to their parents/carers and a few friends to large-scale music festivals. Whatever the size of the event the potential problems tend to be very similar.

I keep a checklist of things to do and one of the great joys in life is ticking them off when you have done them! For bigger events my checklist runs something like this (some of these items might not be necessary for a very small event):

- ☐ **Choose a date**: it's no good planning a concert during a week when the majority of your players are away on a school trip.
  - Will this date give everyone sufficient time to prepare?

- ☐ **The programme**: choosing a balanced and interesting programme featuring a variety of material, styles and different groups does take time to put together but is very worthwhile.
  - Consider having a joint item as bringing together players of different standards can be a major attraction. This is particularly inspiring for young, inexperienced players.
  - Remember to write a programme (or ask someone else). Check it carefully for mistakes or appoint a few proofreaders to do the job for you.

> A word of warning: long concerts are often counter-productive. Think of the poor group who has to go on last when all the audience wants to do is go home or to the pub! Better that the concert ends with the audience wanting more.

- ☐ **The venue**: make sure the venue is suitable for the group(s) that are taking part. How big an audience are you expecting? You must know the capacity of the venue and make sure you do not exceed this. Remember that this includes audience and performers: are there enough chairs for them all?
  - Wherever possible make provision for the participants to sit in and watch the concert when they are not playing.
  - Make a list of all the equipment needed.
  - Will any transport be required? What about moving larger instruments or bags of stands if the concert venue is different from your normal rehearsal room?

> **Health and safety**
> Safety at work is a bigger issue than it was twenty or thirty years ago and most if not all countries will have policies in place reflecting this. It is essential to assess any hazards before and on the day of the concert that may put the participants and audience at risk. Appropriate safeguards must be taken to minimise any such risks. The DfES website (*www.dfes.gov.uk*) is a useful starting point. It is useful and sometimes a requirement to have First Aid facilities at hand.

- ☐ **Organise publicity**: how are you going to advertise the concert? In the local newspaper, on local radio, to friends and family?
  - Remember your invitations to VIPs. Don't forget to invite the headteacher of the school where you are holding the concert.

- ☐ **Information to players and parents/carers**: ignore this at your peril! The last thing you want is a barrage of complaints.
  - Dress code, if any, needs to be decided.
  - Arrival times and rehearsal schedule to be circulated in advance.
  - Parental consent forms may be necessary if students are to leave the premises between the rehearsal and concert.

Tips to help the day go smoothly
- Refreshments are a vital part of musicians' life. Don't skimp! Bring in volunteers to serve drinks and biscuits to musicians and the audience in the interval
- Come armed with the seating plan so that you do not waste valuable time working out where to place the stands
- Organise facilities for changing and put up signs accordingly
- Is there somewhere to lock valuables away while everyone is playing?
- Supervision: vital if different groups are playing and students are in dressing rooms during the concert

> For a large event it is wise to have a stage manager to sort out all the equipment needed for each item. Nominate students to assist the stage manager. This will ensure the concert runs much more smoothly and will allow you to concentrate on the musical items.

The concert

Don't forget health and safety announcements: where fire exits are and so on. This is also an opportune moment to ask everyone to switch off their mobile phones if they have not already done so! Not only is it musically devastating when a mobile goes off but also a source of great embarrassment for the parent concerned. It produces a 'hot flush' at the very least.

Remember to tune up together, even if only slight alterations need to be made. This helps everyone to relax and become a little more familiar with the acoustics. Acoustics can change when an audience is present and sometimes lead you to force the sound unnecessarily.

Relax and enjoy the fruits of all your hard work but don't forget to have helpers organised at the end to help with clearing up. After all, you will be ready for a drink!

Don't forget to congratulate the students on playing so well and thank the audience for coming. Wish everyone a safe journey home and start thinking about the next concert!

Further reading

Score Reading: Orchestration Book 1 Roger Fiske (OUP ISBN 019321301X)

Score Reading: A Key to the Musical Experience Michael Dickreiter (Amadeus Press ISBN 1-57467-056-5)

Nigel Stubbs
GRNCM LRAM Cert.ed
Assistant Head of
Staffordshire Performing
Arts; teacher of violin
and viola

Your teaching career

by Isobel Leibman

As a teacher, you will be regarded as a professional; an expert in your field. It is important to think right from the start of how you present yourself, build your career and develop your own potential to its fullest.

The qualities of a teacher

What qualities do you need to be a successful instrumental/vocal teacher? Whenever this question is posed in an interview situation, one of the most often quoted answers is 'enthusiasm'. That is exactly right, but you will also need competence, qualifications, energy and reliability, as well as superb levels of communication, organisation and time management skills. Quite a profile!

Qualifications and competence
You will obviously need **a high level of ability on your own instrument** and it is ideal if this is reflected by your qualifications. Whatever stage you are at, be it upper grades or degree level, you should consider the benefits of taking a specialist diploma. A teaching diploma will be particularly welcomed and respected by employers, parents/carers/carers and pupils alike.

You will also need **a wide knowledge of repertoire**. Being open minded and using a variety of styles including pop, jazz, and traditional folk styles alongside classical music helps your pupils experience the widest range of music.

Your ability to enthuse: a good lesson should be lively with a fun element, especially at beginner level. Keep your lessons varied, and move the pace along. Do demonstrate to inspire your pupils and let them hear what they are striving for.

Should you learn another instrument? Apart from the obvious advantages of being a pianist, you may well find it an advantage to be able to teach some 'allied instruments', particularly if you specialise in woodwind or brass. For instance, as a clarinettist, being able to teach the flute or saxophone will increase your employment potential. However, do remember that solid technique is extremely important even at beginner level, so you should only teach an instrument which is not your speciality if you are confident in your ability to do it well.

Energy! The life of an instrumental teacher is often fast-paced, involving short lessons, group teaching and multiple school visits in a day. Even if you work at home or in a studio and do not have to travel, you may have to work in the evenings or weekends (which may restrict your social life!).

Reliability: your pupils will look forward to their lessons and will be disappointed if they are cancelled. When building your career, think carefully about how much teaching you can realistically take on without clashing with other commitments.

Be sociable: this is a job where getting on with people is crucial. You will be working with a range of people, including pupils, parents/carers, colleagues, employers and examiners. You will need to communicate with all of them at the right level, so be open, approachable and pleasant.

You may well be teaching groups of pupils together, so **organisational and time management skills** must be good. Lesson plans will be written ahead of time, but registers, pupil progress records and homework diaries must all be completed within the lesson time. This is a challenge, but very beneficial.

Your curriculum vitae

Your CV should be full, accurate and well presented. It is often the first contact you will have with your prospective employer, so it must look good!

Keep it simple and don't be tempted to put in too much. Two sides of A4 paper is usually ample. Be honest about your abilities; show as wide a range of skills as you can without exaggerating and seek permission from referees before you quote them. The format below shows just one way you might like to present your C.V.

Curriculum Vitae
Name (and optional photo)

Personal details:

Address	Email address
Phone numbers	Date of birth

Education history:
List universities, colleges and schools attended, with dates and qualifications: start at the most recent and work back as far as secondary school or equivalent (about age 11).

Employment history:
List places of employment with dates and full details of duties undertaken: start at the present and work back as far as school-leaving (about age 18).

Additional courses attended:
List course titles, subjects and dates (usually within the last two years) with most recent first. Be selective if necessary and only include the most relevant ones.

Other experience/skills:
Voluntary work, etc.

Personal statement:
Make yourself sound interesting and the kind of person who will fit in well with others.

Referees:
Give two; one work and one personal.

Interviews

Interviews vary considerably. Be prepared to play your instrument(s) and possibly to give a short demonstration lesson. Expect questions about yourself and your ambitions, your teaching strategies (motivating pupils, promoting your instrument, repertoire, exams, lesson content) and so on.

The 'Golden Rules' for interviews

- Aim to accept interview dates as offered; only ask for a change in case of real emergency.
- Be prepared: read up on the requirements of the job beforehand and be ready to show how you can meet them.
- Dress smartly – present yourself professionally.
- Smile and greet your prospective employer confidently.
- Show confidence in your ability, but don't be self-opinionated. Keep to the question, don't rush and cover the main points thoroughly.
- Use examples from your own experience (and show any of your own devised worksheets you may have) to illustrate points you make.
- If you don't understand a question, ask for clarification.
- You may be asked if you have any questions, so have a sensible one ready if possible.
- If you are offered the job and you want it, be ready to accept. If you don't want it, give a short reason.
- If you don't get the job, do ask for feedback, and use it in the future.

Setting up as a teacher

So, armed with qualifications, CV and interview technique, you are now ready to build your career. Consider the options, including:

1. Teaching at home or in a studio.
2. Teaching in individual schools.
3. Teaching for a music service or agency who will find work for you.
4. Teaching in an independent music school, college or university.

Securing work needs you to be pro-active. Option 1 will require you to set yourself up in an adequately equipped teaching room at home or in a rented studio and advertise for pupils. This can take time to begin with, but you can soon find yourself with quite a waiting list, once your reputation builds.

For options 2, 3 and 4, you will need to look out for advertisements. These are often found in local and national newspapers and specialist periodicals. The internet is another good source of information. You can also try writing speculative letters. Remember, you can send your C.V. direct to schools or organisations in your area by post or email.

Option 4 will be looking for the very best music teachers, and competition will be fierce. Sometimes ex-students can secure work in establishments they attended as students. Often institutions will choose teachers with substantial performing careers to provide an experienced role model for students.

Equipment and facilities for the private teacher

Give some thought to the equipment and facilities you will need:

- **The teaching room**: if you are providing a teaching room, consider its suitability for the purpose. If at your house, is it a designated practice room? Can it be family-free while you are teaching so that you can give total concentration to your pupils without interruption? You should consider how you lay the room out. There should be adequate heat and light and it should be tidy. There should be sufficient space for you and your pupils to feel comfortable and you should take care to position yourself so that you are in view whilst teaching.
- **Instruments and equipment**: you will of course need your own

instrument and if you are providing an instrument for your pupil to use (e.g. piano or drum kit), make sure it is of a good enough quality. There is a huge range of equipment you can collect to help you, but this really depends on how much travelling around you have to do. Essentials include music stands, pencils, rhythm flash cards, manuscript paper, note books and pupil records. Additionally you could have a metronome, tuning fork, Cd player, perhaps even a recordable mini-disk.

- **Music**: build up a range of music, including favourite exam pieces, technical exercises and other pieces to extend your pupils' abilities. File them clearly and logically and include sight-reading and ensemble pieces appropriate to your pupils' age and ability range.
- **Examinations**: will probably be an integral part of your pupils' progress, so you will need examination syllabi and entry forms to help you get organised. You will find these at most music shops, or they can be posted to you direct.
- **Dress appropriately**: it is important to look professional.
- **Time keeping**: start and end lessons promptly, leaving enough time to complete your records with your pupils at the end of the lesson and see them in and out of the building if necessary. If pupils are late, don't be tempted to keep them beyond their time – it could make lessons run late for everyone else!
- **Record keeping**: is essential. The basic necessities are pupil and school contact details, registers, teaching plans and records, exam results and your own records (for tax purposes and so on). Building a profile of each pupil which tracks their progress, showing exam dates and results and concert performances is a nice personal touch. It can be passed on to pupils when they leave and can be shown at future interviews to show the scope of your teaching experience.

> Hopefully, you will get started in your teaching career without too much trouble, but there will always be issues and queries. Do join a professional organisation to support you, and get to know other teachers in your area who may be more experienced and can offer you sound advice.

Your career development

Now that you have started on your teaching career, you will want to think about the future. You need to build a reputation as an excellent teacher, and you will want to make sure that your own skills continue to be developed. It all takes energy and determination, but there are lots of rewarding areas to pursue.

Advertising and promoting yourself

Advertise in local papers and music shops; personal web sites are useful, too – a well-designed one can look very exciting. Include qualifications, areas of special interest or expertise, examination successes and a short biography. Your reputation will spread by word of mouth too, and recommendations from pupils are very powerful. If you work for an organisation, let your employer know you are keen to take on more teaching and involve yourself as fully as you can. Being flexible and offering to help out always impresses and makes you feel part of the team.

Recruiting in schools

In schools, you will still need boundless energy to recruit, but the strategies you use will vary to fit in with school policies. Hopefully, there will already be some prospective pupils eagerly waiting to learn, so you need to speak to the school and discuss recruiting strategies. You could arrange a short demonstration concert to a class of children. Play pieces that the children will know and like (current pop tunes or TV themes) and invite them to join in by singing or clapping along. Pupils often want to play an instrument because their friends do, so ask any existing pupils at the school to join in.

Examinations

Exam results will probably form part of the foundation of your reputation. They are one clear way of showing progress and achievement, but you do need to think carefully about how to manage them.

Grades should fit snugly into your overall planning, with pupils taking them only when they are thoroughly prepared. Many new teachers worry about gauging the standard for entry. The best advice is aim high, but be realistic and do pay equal attention to ALL sections of the exam. Many examination boards also provide details of their assessment criteria which may be a useful starting point.

- **Allow 'growing time'** between grades for repertoire building and extension work such as improvisation. Spread grades out so that pupils take them at an age of appropriate musical maturity. Pupils or parents/carers/carers may try to exert pressure for exams to be taken quickly. If you disagree, say so and give reasons. You are the expert and failure can be very damaging. Remember: it's not a race!
- **Add variety!** With so much flexibility available now, it is easy to vary the format to suit pupils' needs. All grades include different options such as technical work instead of scales, or composing your own piece to perform in the exam.

Pupils' concerts

Celebrate success and provide a showcase. Include all your pupils, perhaps particularly featuring 'high scorers'. It is motivating for the pupils and parents/carers will be impressed by their children's achievements and your initiative in providing a platform for them. Consider hiring a small hall, and charging entry to cover costs. Do check that relevant insurance and health and safety issues are in order though.

> **The three P's: pleasant, punctual and professional.**
> Keep these at the front of your mind and you will go far!

Continuing professional development

Once you are qualified and have built up your teaching practice, you should think about your continuing professional development (CPD). Musicians often base their teaching on how they themselves were taught. This is fine, particularly if you had an inspiring teacher. However, methods

*change and the range of music activities being taught is becoming ever
more exciting and varied. There are many courses available which can
help you broaden your knowledge and feel more confident.*

Higher level diplomas

More teaching can mean less practice but maintaining your own playing
standard is vital. You can build your performing skills and competence
through studying for a higher-level diploma (such as the recital-based FTCL).

Broadening your teaching skills

Trinity's 'Profile' offers a number of courses to extend your teaching skills.
You may even be inspired to change direction with your career. Early years
music for the under fives, for instance, is an area where specialist knowledge
is crucial to success. You may find that you can set up a thriving pre-school
music club, laying down excellent foundations for music in the very young
child. Other options include jazz or music technology. It is always exciting
to find a new skill and with the support of a comprehensive training
programme, you really can do something different!

If you are working for an organisation you can find out about CPD
opportunities by:
- Asking if you can go on a course and pass skills on by training others.
- Enquiring if your employer might host a training session for
  employees. In some cases there is no charge.
- Asking about in-house training, including opportunities to observe
  lessons given by more experienced teachers.
- Offering to lead a training session yourself on a subject you have
  specialist knowledge in. This will develop your own skills as well as
  those of your trainees.

If you are working independently, find out about CPD opportunities by:
- Getting together with other music teachers with the same interests and
  share costs.
- Joining a professional organisation for your instrument who will send
  information regularly or subscribing to a specialist magazine.
- Looking out for new publications which will keep you in touch with
  new initiatives.

Your extended career

Once you are well-established as a teacher, you may like to extend your
career into co-ordinating or managing. Consider the following:
- Within schools, music services or agencies you may be able to move to
  more senior posts over time. These may involve managing other
  teachers: an exciting position where team-building, mentoring and
  motivating skills will be required.
- As an independent teacher, develop a high profile in the locality. If you
  have facilities, you could set yourself up as an examination centre for
  your own pupils and those of local teachers.
- Independent schools sometimes advertise for senior staff such as a
  Head of Strings. Duties may include responsibility for junior staff and
  possibly ensemble directorship.
- Start a local ensemble.

- Offer to adjudicate at festivals.
- Apply to become an examiner.

These are examples of extended career opportunities for good musicians, which sit well alongside teaching. Over time, as you become more skilled as a teacher and you build a solid reputation for good results, you may want to use your own knowledge to help others. Or you may wish to develop skills in other areas of music education such as composition. Either way, there are courses and diplomas in these and other fields and it is worth remembering that qualifications like these will also be much valued by employers seeking staff with management and leadership potential.

The rules

Policies within an organisation
If you are working for an organisation, you will probably find that there are structures and policies already in place in the form of a code of conduct or staff handbook. This is likely to include details and procedures for signing in at schools, registers, absences (for pupils and teachers), examination entry, health and safety, and so on. You must take care to read this and follow 'the rules'. Your employer will have high expectations of you as a representative of the organisation, so remember: pleasant, punctual and professional!

Policy-setting for your own private practice
If you are setting up your own independent teaching practice, you will have the flexibility to set your own hours and conditions for working. Think carefully about setting ground rules. This will help avoid misunderstandings over agreements and expectations. Consider devising a prospectus for pupils setting out working practices. This might include:
- A short biography: your training, qualifications and experience.
- Your charging policy and terms and conditions: lesson rates, how you charge (weekly or by invoice at the start or end of term), discounts for siblings, rules for notice of termination (often one month or a term in advance) and rules for non-attendance (which may be payment due in full if 24 hours notice is not given).
- Term dates.
- Policy on parents/carers attending lessons (perhaps for younger pupils only).
- Free 'no-obligation first lesson' giving you and your pupil a chance to see if you will get along.
- Information on possible open lessons or pupil concerts.
- Practice expectations: how long and how often.
- Examination entry procedure (on your recommendation).
- Policy for written reports (usually annually) and parental liaison time (perhaps by telephone at an agreed time).
- Necessity for prompt collection of children at the end of lessons.

Responsibilities

There is a range of responsibility issues relating to employment as a teacher either independently or for an organisation. Working conditions and rules vary worldwide and you should always seek expert advice from the relevant authorities in your area. The issues highlighted below will alert you to the fact that as a teacher, it is your responsibility to be aware of such issues, to seek advice and to act appropriately.

Employment status

When setting up independently or working for an organisation, you must take responsibility for keeping accurate records of all your earnings and expenses. Keep all receipts, copies of invoices and any other proof of income or employment-related expenditure. This is for tax and other purposes as appropriate where proof of income is needed. If unsure, you should seek advice from a suitably qualified accountant, who understands employment and tax issues as they apply to you.

Insurance

We live in a litigious age and in the event of an accident or incident occurring the injured party will often attempt to apportion blame to any one but themselves and seek compensation.

If you are setting up independently, you will need appropriate Public Liability insurance cover with an adequate limit of indemnity for any one accident or incident for yourself and your clients. Again, you will need to seek advice from an expert in this respect (such as your accountant or an insurance broker familiar with liability insurance) to ensure that the cover is adequate for your circumstances. If you are being employed by an organisation, ask them about the scope of insurance cover provided by their organisation for all aspects of your duties before you commence your employment.

Terms of employment

If you are undertaking teaching for an organisation, you need to be clear on what is expected of you as conditions of employment do differ. Your future employer should set out the terms and conditions clearly for you at interview. However, if you are unsure, seeking clarification at least on the following will help avoid misunderstandings later:

- Terms and conditions of your employment (contracted or sessional)?
- Are hours constant or variable?
- Are you entitled to sick pay and holiday pay?
- What is the expected duration of the employment?
- How much, when, and how will you be paid (by cheque or directly into your bank account) and are there claim forms to complete?
- Can travel costs be claimed back?
- Is there a pension scheme?

Data protection

As a teacher, you may be in possession of your pupils' personal information such as addresses, telephone numbers and reports. It is most important to understand that these records are likely to be covered by the Data Protection Act. The safe rule is 'do not pass these on to any other party', however, for complete understanding of these issues, expert advice on Data Protection in your area should be sought from a professional association.

Child protection

This is a sensitive and wide-ranging issue and teachers would be well advised to find out how child protection legislation might have implications for their work. These days we are all much more aware of the sensitivities of children being on their own with an adult who is not their parent. Indeed, an accusation of inappropriate behaviour on the part of the teacher, even if it is a false one, can end a teaching career. The relationship between an instrumental or vocal teacher and their students is a unique one and demands particularly sensitive handling. Here are some suggestions for ways of avoiding problems from the start:

- *Physical contact*: some teachers find it impossible to teach without some kind of physical guidance being provided. This should be kept to a minimum, limited to the arms only and the student's permission should always be sought. Try to demonstate posture yourself and ask the pupil to copy, rather than using physical contact. Give your pupils space: don't stand too close and crowd them.

- *Teaching room*: Teach where you can be seen and heard by others if possible. A room with a window or viewing panel in the door is best, or try leaving the door open while you teach if you can.

- *Conversation*: every instrumental teacher wants to have a relaxed relationship with their students and conversations will often cover issues outside the lesson. When dealing with issues of posture, mouth position and so on, phrase your sentences carefully and be clear and unambiguous. Never stray into areas of personal relationships – yours or your students' – and never make comments which could be taken personally or cause offence.

- *Crushes*: the cliché of the teenager who develops a crush on their instrumental teacher is not an uncommon occurrence. If you suspect something like this is happening talk to someone about it – either the parents/carers or the school. At all times keep a professional distance between yourself and your pupils.

- *Personal problems*: it is not unknown for students to use the instrumental lesson as an outlet to talk to someone about problems they are experiencing. In these cases the teacher should use their professional judgement to determine whether this is something that can be played down or whether it is a more serious issue (such as bullying, difficulties at home, drugs, and so on).
  - Do not try to elicit more information than is given.
  - Make accurate notes of what was said immediately after the lesson.
  - Follow the advice given by the school or organisation: contact the headteacher of the school or organisation who will direct you to the member of staff with responsibility for these issues.
  - Do not disclose information or discuss the matter with anyone else.
  - If you are working independently contact your union or professional organisation immediately for advice.

Isobel Liebman
BA Hons, ARCM,
AMusTCL, CertEd
Principle of Havering
Music School
(LEA Music Service)

Further reading and information

Keeping Your Nerve! Kate Jones (Faber Music 0-571-51922-9)
A very useful little book on how to combat performance nerves.

Compose Yourself! Paul Harris and Robert Tucker (Faber Music 0-571-51990-3)
Good ideas on how to get pupils composing.

Music Teacher magazine (Rhinegold Publishing) www.rhinegold.co.uk
A very informative magazine, which regularly has a focus on a particular discipline (e.g. strings or jazz).

Classical Music magazine (Rhinegold Publishing) www.rhinegold.co.uk
Monthly magazine which will keep you up to date. Often features articles about composers or musical institutions. Also advertises vacancies (often quite prestigious ones).

A Common Approach
A good solid curriculum for the instrumental teacher. Comes with a generic section and an instrument family specific one. Available from The Federation of Music Services (see below).

The National Association of Music Educators (NAME) www.name2.org.uk
This website has a substantial amount of links to other useful sites.

The Federation of Music Services (FMS) www.federationmusic.org.uk
This website has some interesting information on LEA Music Services including 'How to find a good teacher'. There is also a 'Vacancies' section and contact details for Music Services across England, Wales and Northern Ireland.

Trinity's Music Diplomas

Trinity examinations are known all over the world for the quality of the experience and the value that they offer candidates. The extended range of diplomas are vocationally focused and offer great variety, appealing to all areas of the music profession. You can opt for performance-only recital diplomas or diplomas including written work and there is a completely revised and modernised range of teaching qualifications. Other subject areas include mentoring, assessment, directing and composing.

There are three levels of diploma qualifications: Associate (ATCL), Licentiate (LTCL) and Fellowship (FTCL). The Trinity suite encourages you to progress through the diplomas, chosing the right level and the right focus for your career development and personal goals.

Trinity offers diplomas which are one-off assessments; however, most consist of a combination of units to allow you to demonstrate your ability in a variety of ways. These fall in to three main categories:
- Performance or practical demonstration
- Written examination
- Submitted materials and discussion of these with an examiner

These are the qualifications that will prove you have the skills necessary to progress along your chosen professional path.

Diplomas available:	Associate	Licentiate	Fellowship
Performance			
Performance including technical components	ATCL	LTCL	FTCL
Recital	ATCL	LTCL	
Music Practice: Performing	ATCL	LTCL	FTCL
Teaching and Directing, Mentoring and Assessment			
Instrumental/Vocal Teaching	ATCL	LTCL	
Specialist Music Teaching for Groups	ATCL	LTCL	
Music Facilitating	ATCL	LTCL	FTCL
Music Education			FTCL
Music Practice: Mentoring	ATCL	LTCL	
Music Practice: Adjudicating		LTCL	FTCL
Music Practice: Directing	ATCL	LTCL	
Music Direction			FTCL
Theory and Composition			
Music Literacy	AMusTCL	LMusTCL	FMusTCL
Music Composition		LTCL	FTCL
Music Practice: Composing	ATCL	LTCL	FTCL

For further information about Trinity's music diplomas, including application forms, fee information, centre details and downloadable syllabuses, visit the Trinity website at www.trinitycollege.co.uk or contact:

Trinity College *London*, 89 Albert Embankment
London SE1 7TP, United Kingdom
Tel: +44 (0) 20 7820 6100   Fax: +44 (0) 20 7820 6161
Email: music@trinitycollege.co.uk